ENTREPRENEURIAL LEADERSHIP

ENTREPRENEURIAL LEADERSHIP

A Practical Guide to Generating New Business

ANGELO MASTRANGELO

 PRAEGER ™

An Imprint of ABC-CLIO, LLC

Santa Barbara, California • Denver, Colorado

Library of Congress Cataloging-in-Publication Data

Mastrangelo, Angelo, author.
    Entrepreneurial leadership : a practical guide to generating new business / Angelo Mastrangelo.
        pages cm
    Includes bibliographical references and index.
    ISBN 978-1-4408-3554-4 (print : alk. paper) — ISBN 978-1-4408-3555-1 (e-book)
1. New business enterprises—Management. 2. Leadership. 3. Entrepreneurship.
4. Strategic planning. I. Title.
    HD62.5.M3658 2016
    658.4'21—dc23   2015028278

ISBN: 978-1-4408-3554-4
EISBN: 978-1-4408-3555-1

20   19   18   17   3   4   5

This book is also available on the World Wide Web as an eBook.
Visit www.abc-clio.com for details.

Praeger
An Imprint of ABC-CLIO, LLC

ABC-CLIO, LLC
130 Cremona Drive, P.O. Box 1911
Santa Barbara, California 93116-1911

This book is printed on acid-free paper ∞

Manufactured in the United States of America

Contents

Acknowledgments

Never in my life did I think I'd write a book. While at times it's been painful, it's also given me a wonderful opportunity to "take stock" of those who've made a difference in my life. In no particular order, I'd like to thank:

My family: My mother and father, who did a great job of keeping the family together. My four brothers, Al, Marv, Joe, and Tony, who are always there for me. My grandfather Mariano, who was my hero when I still believed in heroes. My children, Diane (Dee), Scott, Michele (Shelly), and Angelo Joseph (AJ), who motivated me and made me proud throughout my life, as well as their children, Ryan, Amanda, Jake, Grace, Nathan, and Nina. My great-grandchildren, Clara and Adele. I would be remiss to leave out my two wonderful friends and in-laws, Ralph and Katherine Arnold.

All my friends at Adirondack, including Carl Touhey, who gave me my first opportunity in leadership and provided mentorship, as well as Frank Cosenza, Doug Martin, and Veronica Mattas. At Harvard, Marty Marshall, By Barnes, Phil Thurston, and Jackie Baugher.

At Albany University: Dianna Stone, who lobbied to have me accepted in the Organizational Studies PhD program and became a friend. Cecelia Falbe, Kevin Williams, Paul Miesing, and a special thanks to my advisor and friend Jim Jaccard, who was most responsible for my earning a PhD.

At Binghamton University: Upinder Dhillon, who asked me to start the entrepreneurship program and who has fully supported the program and me ever since. George Bobinski, Shelly Dionne, Kim Jaussi, and Fran Yammarino (thanks for the tip on the title), Alesia Wheeler, Debbie Bundy, Brian Perry, Debbie Standard, and Rachel Coker, whose suggestion set in motion my writing this book. My regular guest speakers for my class, Arel Moodie, Bert Gervais, Dave Maione, Anthony Paniccia, and Ian Bel. A very special thanks to all my students: I'm not going to name any in fear of offending the ones I left out.

The board members of the Second Chance Scholarship Program: Father Chris DeGiovine (a good friend and human being), John Kucij, Jack Beckett, John Smircich, Jeanne Kobuszewski, Phil Johnson, Susan Patterson, Cathy Hans, Fred Stein, our first executive director, Dominick Eanello, and our attorney, Jack Clark. All our donors, especially Marc Newman, Warren Hill, James Cahill, Ben Zuckerman, and Dan Nolan. A special thanks to all of the people who administrate our program and support us at our participating schools and their foundations, Hudson Valley Community College, The College of St. Rose, Albany University, SUNY Broome, and Delhi University.

The "special people" who fall into more than one category: My colleagues and coauthors Steve Lorenz and Erik Eddy, who have added a great deal to our research and publications. Erik also for his contributions as executive director of our foundation and for being a good friend. Mark Hartman, who convinced his company to finance the purchase of our company and who was a valuable supporter and is a good friend. My friend Carl Sloane, who motivated me to seek my PhD, and who has helped and supported me ever since. Monsignor Paul Brigandi, whom I have known for much of my life and who has been my spiritual mentor, supporter, and close friend. Finally my business mentor, Al DiPasqua, who coached me through the purchase of Adirondack Beverages and is the best partner a person could ever have.

A very special thanks to my editor, Tricia Parker, for all your guidance, help, and assistance. This book would never have been possible or for that matter worth reading without your invaluable assistance. You are the best.

Finally it is always good to leave the best for last. Thanks to my lovely wife, Kathy, who has loved and supported me through thick and thin and is the best thing that ever happened to me. To her I dedicate this book.

Prologue

Defining Entrepreneurial Leadership

On Friday the thirteenth of June 1980, after 11 months of negotiating and pursuing financing, I finally acquired Adirondack Beverages (formerly Bev-Pak), a multimillion-dollar soft-drink manufacturing company in New York State, from IT&T. At the time I was a plant manager at Bev-Pak, a division of IT&T, which was the 11th-largest company in the world when IT&T purchased it in 1976. As I sat at a table in Philadelphia surrounded by lawyers, accountants, and executives, I pictured my Italian grandfather saying, "Oh-nah-ly in America couldda you do dis, Angelo."

There was certainly an echo of truth in this. I had $232.00 in my checking account, a zero balance in my savings account, and credit cards with exhausted credit limits. I was so short on cash that my lawyer had to pay for the airfare, hotel rooms, and meals. It didn't help that I had little formal education (a high school degree and a year of nights at a community college), no power, and no friends in influential places. What I did have was 20 years in the beverage industry, my reputation, customers who trusted me, and a lot of people who believed in me. I'm proud to say that 35 years after I bought the company, Adirondack is still thriving today.

When I purchased Bev-Pak and renamed it Adirondack Beverages, the company was by no means prospering: in the 11 months of negotiating, the owners had "chased away" 60 percent of their sales volume with poor service. The company's monthly losses were in the six-figure range. Amazingly, the owners weren't concerned: they'd decided that if by the end of 1980 they didn't consummate a sale, the company would be shut down and liquidated.

Economic conditions in the country weren't much better, and interest rates had skyrocketed. The prime rate had reached an all-time high of 18 percent. In early 1980 the country went into a deep recession, caused in part by a large round of oil price increases set off by turmoil in Iran. Compounding the situation was an ongoing crisis in the soft drink industry. U.S. soft drink consumption was at an all-time high, but Coke and Pepsi's "mega-plants" were squeezing both major brands and the little guys out. At the end of the sixties, U.S. beverage plants numbered about 6,000; now we were down to fewer than 1,600. Beverage industry experts predicted that only 200 plants would be standing by the end of the century.

Despite all this, I was confident that we could turn the company around. Bev-Pak had done well before being purchased by ITT. I was Bev-Pak's general manager at the time, so I knew our customers and our people inside out. I knew what had worked in the past and what the previous owners had done to bring the company to its current situation. I had a plan to turn it around. With 20 years in the business, respect for our employees, and the goodwill of our customers, I was prepared to take on this challenge. I was determined to be one of the "last 200" plants standing.

Being on the front lines of the Cola Wars—and ultimately winning our battle—taught me that successfully leading a company out of crisis takes more than just a "normal" style of leadership. It takes a special form of leadership, which I call "entrepreneurial leadership." In this book, I'll discuss how entrepreneurial leadership can be applied to all types of organizations regardless of size, ownership, or profit or nonprofit status, in times of both crisis and stability.

This special form of leadership begins with the creative process often referred to as "being entrepreneurial." This process is often characterized by taking financial risks in the hope of making a profit, or "being enterprising." Entrepreneurship, however, is much more than this; it is a process whose purpose is to generate new business. "Business," for the purposes of our discussion, is defined as "products, services, and the organizations needed to deliver them." The process starts with the ability to recognize an opportunity worth pursuing and knowing what is needed to bring it to market and make it successful: the focus of the first part of the book.

Knowing how to generate new business, however, is never enough; doing it demands the ability to lead. Persuading your people to buy into the opportunity, cooperate willingly, and making the opportunity real and successful requires professional and personal leadership, the topic of the second half of the book. The principles of professional and personal leadership are still what guide Adirondack Beverages today.

Unlike other forms of leadership, whose sole aim might be to govern, educate, and protect, entrepreneurial leadership exists to generate new business. All organizations, regardless of type, need to provide products and services to grow and survive. Business is not only good for the economy; it is also the engine that keeps it moving and growing. Entrepreneurs are—and always have been—the major generators of business.

In this book, I present easy-to-understand models of both entrepreneurship and leadership, keeping in mind that entrepreneurial leaders first and foremost generate new business.

* * *

As a preliminary measure, the good entrepreneurial leader realizes that—contrary to what might be the prevailing business ethos—the art of generating new business is selfless, and not selfish. He or she understands that the business world should be a "you" world, not a "we" or "me" world. By that I mean that good entrepreneurial leaders focus on the needs and wants of the consumer, knowing that by satisfying the consumer first, the "we" and "me" will benefit later.

Often, I've heard aspiring entrepreneurs referred to as "dreamers." Yet up-and-coming entrepreneurial leaders are not dreamers, nor for that matter high-risk takers. They are visionaries who are goal oriented and who take calculated risks. I define a goal as "a dream with an achievable plan." Successful entrepreneurial leaders always have effective plans by which they can achieve their goals. They are long-term, rather than short-term, thinkers.

In the words of Steve Case, cofounder of AOL, "The great entrepreneurs that really have had a significant impact in the world take a long-term-view. They really think of it in decades, not years or months. They really believe that in the long run they're going to have a tremendous impact."[1]

Amazon.com founder Jeff Bezos also emphasizes the importance of long-term thinking. "If everything you do needs to work on a three-year time horizon, then you're competing against a lot of people," Bezos told *Wired* magazine in 2011. "But if you're willing to invest on a seven-year time horizon, you're now competing against a fraction of those people, because very few companies are willing to do that."[2]

Since entrepreneurial leaders are "bred," not born, entrepreneurial leadership is a *process* that must be learned over time. My Opportunity and Enduring Leadership models, which constitute parts I and II of the book, will show you how to learn this process.

I have a good idea . . . if only it were me! This is the mantra of most every beginning entrepreneur. However, most ideas aren't business-generating opportunities, and looking for opportunities through one's own ideas most often ends up in frustration. In the Opportunity Model (chapters 1–5), we'll explore how to differentiate between an idea and the ever-elusive, potentially profitable opportunity. We'll also explore what is needed to make it successful.

My Enduring Leadership Model (chapters 6–9) will teach you how to be an effective leader, based on my more than 35 years as a successful entrepreneur. We'll first learn about the importance of inspiring passion and vision in the people you'll be leading, whom I call "co-operators." Then we'll take a look at how bureaucracy—Max Weber's "iron cage of rationality"—stifles entrepreneurship, using some amusing examples.

Finally, we'll explore the interplay between what I call "professional leadership"—leadership that provides direction, processes, and coordination—and "personal leadership," which is centered on the more "human" elements of expertise, trust, caring, sharing, and morality. We'll end the book with examples of how to be an entrepreneurial leader in non-business settings, and we'll take a look at some of the "enduring relationship" lessons I've learned time and again.

* * *

Throughout the 20th and 21st centuries, scholars have struggled to define the concept of "entrepreneurial leadership." Joseph Schumpeter, one of the most influential economists of the 20th century, noted that entrepreneurship itself had no fewer than five "forms." These included, among others, "the introduction of a new method of production," "the exploitation of a new source of supply," and the "re-engineering of business management practices."[3]

Other scholars fell on the opposite side of the line, oversimplifying the concept of entrepreneurship. Entrepreneurship, said Ludwig von Mises, one of the last members of the original Austrian School of economics, is the driving force of the market—that is to say, of civilized society[4]—while entrepreneurship professor William B. Gartner defined it as "the creation of new organizations."[5]

The business press joins in with its one-liners: "Entrepreneurship . . . involves the creation of something new," said a 2014 *Forbes* article.[6] Says another *Forbes* article written around that time, "One of the defining traits of an entrepreneur is the ability to take an idea and make it better."[7]

Fourteen years ago, having sold Adirondack Beverages back in 1993, I started teaching leadership in the MBA program at New York State's Binghamton University. Eighteen months into the program, the dean asked me to start an entrepreneurship program, beginning with a class for both undergraduate and graduate students.

Despite my background in leadership and practicing entrepreneurship, I was at a loss for how to begin teaching what seemed to me like a huge, complex topic. What was it, exactly, that I wanted my students to learn? What was the single most important message I could impart after my 13 years of running a multimillion-dollar company, and heading up three major turnarounds?

I started by reaching out to some professors I knew at world-renowned Babson College, Julian Lange and Bill Bygraves, as well as a Harvard friend, Carl Sloane. Carl was a leadership professor in Harvard's MBA program. He'd become a heavyweight in his field in a very short period of time after selling a large Boston consulting firm that he had cofounded. Bill gave me a book of syllabi, and Carl provided me with helpful business cases to study, along with much-appreciated advice. The materials helped me greatly, but I realized a critical element was still missing.

After much trial and error, I discovered that the missing piece was the fact that modern entrepreneurial leadership itself first had to be defined.

Entrepreneurial leadership is not, as many people seem to believe, just the ability to form an organization. No, entrepreneurial leadership is much more than creating start-ups. It is a *process* whose purpose is *generating new business*. The process involves recognizing an opportunity to pursue and forming a team and an organization to deliver it, keeping in mind that entrepreneurial leaders are the driving force behind generating new business. There it was! As soon as I'd defined entrepreneurship, my five-step Opportunity Model—part I of this book—fell into place. It highlights the *process* of *generating new business*. This process isn't confined to privately owned companies, publicly traded companies, or nonprofits. It's certainly not confined to companies just starting out, either. Entrepreneurial leadership is vital to all forms of organizations at all stages of their development. Entrepreneurial leaders are the driving force behind generating new business, and all organizations need new business to sustain themselves and grow.

* * *

The process of generating new business always starts with an idea and a lone individual. I started generating new business as a 26-year-old supervisor at Canada Dry of Southern New York. The company was a franchise bottler, which meant it obtained the rights from a major national brand (also known as the parent company, in the beverage industry) to manufacture and distribute its branded products.

It was one of many holdings of Touhey Associates, owned by Carl Touhey, a businessman from Albany who'd eventually become a trusted mentor. His companies included six franchised soft-drink bottling companies and one contract soft-drink bottling company, which produced store brands and branded products for other companies.

While working for Carl, I developed unique pricing strategies and designed catchy "point-of-purchase" materials. The net result of my efforts was a 35 percent increase in business the first year they were introduced. From that point on, I never stopped generating new business throughout my career.

With each new promotion, the process of generating new business grew easier. When I eventually became owner of Adirondack Beverages, I helped our people develop a highly effective new-product program, a program that is the basis of my Opportunity Model.

I've been refining the Opportunity Model for 13 years now, mostly through student feedback and additional academic materials I've read. I'm confident that the model can be applied to any venture in the world, and that every one of these ventures would benefit by having an entrepreneurial leader in its ranks.

I'm certainly not alone in believing that entrepreneurial leadership is needed by all organizations regardless of size, or whether they're profit or nonprofit. In his book *Innovation and Entrepreneurship*, renowned business expert Peter F. Drucker stresses that existing businesses, especially large ones, are effective at managing but need to learn how to be more entrepreneurial. He also cautions that entrepreneurs just starting out often lack critical management skills:

> The existing business, to oversimplify, knows how to manage but needs to learn how to be entrepreneurial and how to innovate. The non-business public-service institution too faces different problems, has different needs, and is prone to different mistakes. And the new venture needs to learn how to manage.[8]

He emphasizes the need for a better understanding of entrepreneurship and "models of how to do it successfully." He explains that entrepreneurship is "risky" because "so few of the so-called entrepreneurs know what they are doing."[9]

A practical guide for entrepreneurial leaders has never been more necessary. More than 1,500 U.S. colleges and universities now offer some kind of entrepreneurship program, compared with just 400 in 1995. (In 1970, fewer than 20 schools offered any kind of entrepreneurship program at all!) According to a recent report, nearly 80 percent of would-be entrepreneurs in the United States are millennials, or those born from approximately 1980 to 1994.

"[Millennials are] enthusiastic about entrepreneurship. . . . They recognize that entrepreneurship is the key to reviving the economy," said a 2011 report funded by the Ewing Marion Kauffman Foundation in Kansas City.[10] Certainly, a tight job market, witnessing family members lose jobs after decades of service to a company, the Internet, and the success of young entrepreneurs like Facebook founder Mark Zuckerberg have all impacted this influential group.

Still, no matter what age business owners might be, entrepreneurial leadership remains an extremely important subject for *all* Americans. According to the Small Business Administration (SBA), small businesses have provided two-thirds of all new jobs in this country since the 1970s. The small business sector is growing rapidly, with the number of small businesses in the United States increasing by nearly half since 1982.

Sadly, the failure rate of U.S. start-ups remains staggering, at more than 50 percent. Cleary, many entrepreneurial leaders are still in need of a practical compass. That's where my Opportunity Model and my "lessons from the Cola Wars" come in.

My students and I use the model to evaluate every case study we discuss in my class. Many times, after completing my class, students e-mail me, asking for information about the model, telling me they use it all the time. I've yet to find one company that the Opportunity Model can't properly evaluate.

I used the exact same process to develop my Enduring Leadership Model, part II in this book. I based it on a pamphlet we developed at Adirondack called "The Pursuit of Excellence: A Lifelong Journey" (Appendix A). "The Pursuit of Excellence" came at a time of crisis, when we were forced to implement "total quality management" (TQM) programs in order to stay competitive. It was a powerful document that's still in use today. For the first time, it put into words *how* we'd develop trust and credibility, and our "rules" for operating as a company with integrity.

A word about the "how"—many people who teach entrepreneurship gravitate toward the "how," or more specifically a *theory* of the *process* of entrepreneurial leadership. In many cases these instructors use theories developed by others that are based on observation and research, not practical experience and success as an entrepreneurial leader.

Having practiced and studied entrepreneurial leadership, I start off differently. I start with the "what" and the "why." The "what"—generating business—is where all lessons on entrepreneurial leadership should start, and the "why" tells us the reason that generating new business is so darn important. Business is the engine that keeps an economy going and growing. It is also the greatest job provider!

When it comes to the "how," or other instructors' definitions of entrepreneurial leadership, these definitions are often based on how others have been successful entrepreneurs. What they don't tell us is how to generate new business and be successful entrepreneurial leaders. This is what my models will provide for you.

This book bridges the gap between academia and business, "business theory" and the real world. By letting you in on my own failures and successes managing Adirondack Beverages (a company that's about to celebrate its 50th year!), I'll provide you with a time-tested road map to ensure *your* organization's success. Again, this isn't just theoretical: I've been down in my company's trenches, literally "cleaning the factory floor."

I started in the soft drink business as a route salesman, a job that required me to make as many as 60 stops a day. As a sales supervisor, I often found myself rolling up my sleeves and building huge grocery store displays myself. Later, as a general manager, I stacked cases for an entire eight-hour shift in order to prevent shutting down the line. Even when I owned my own company, I'd make sales calls right along with our regional sales managers, just to show them that I'd never ask them to do something I wouldn't do myself. In none of my positions was I above "getting my hands dirty" and making sacrifices on a regular basis.

Yet I've also devoted hundreds of hours to studying the "what" and "why" of my successes—the models or theories behind my time running Adirondack Beverages. I've done this for readers who might already be in the business world and need help addressing persistent, underlying issues.

So, there's a little bit in this book for everyone: for the student interested in becoming an entrepreneur, for the entrepreneurial leader in need of advice, and, well . . . for everyone else. Are you one of the 136,000,000 Americans interested in entrepreneurship? If so, I welcome you on this journey! We hope to prove Mr. Drucker's words wrong—that entrepreneurial leaders *can* know what they're doing, as long as they have a good guide.

Now, let's take a look at where all entrepreneurial leadership should begin, and that is with recognizing an *opportunity*.

Part I

THE OPPORTUNITY MODEL

Introduction to the Opportunity Model

If you're one of the growing numbers of people interested in becoming an entrepreneurial leader, my five-step Opportunity Model will provide you with a time-tested process to help you realize your dreams.

Where Do I Begin?

The entrepreneurial process begins with recognizing an *opportunity*, which is the chance to create a product, service, or organization and successfully bring it to market. Recognizing an opportunity can happen in the start-up stage, or in the midst of a well-established company or organization. The most critical thing an entrepreneurial leader must know how to do is recognize an *opportunity worth pursuing*. Pursuing ideas that are not real opportunities is a sure path to failure, as we'll soon see in the next chapter.

In the grocery industry in the 1990s, 30,000 new products were introduced each year. Considering that supermarkets carried only 25,000 items each, the success rate of new products was less than 1 percent. Yet at Adirondack Beverages, where I was CEO, our new product success rate was over 90 percent. How was this the case?

The answer lies in my five-step Opportunity Model, which I developed after many years of working in the highly competitive grocery industry. With my team's help, we tested, implemented, and improved a model that I've used all throughout my career as a successful entrepreneur.

The five steps of my "Opportunity Model" are as follows:

1. Identify a Commercially Viable Problem

The problem you identify must be *ready* to be solved, and the solution to the problem must be commercially viable. In other words, there must be a large enough demand for a solution if the product or service is to be commercially viable.

2. Create a Product or Service That Has a Strong Competitive and Comparative Advantage

Your product or service must be unique, in that it must be positioned as better in some way than existing products and services. Securing effective distribution channels, as well as creating awareness for your product or service, is also essential to achieving a competitive and comparative advantage.

3. Ensure That Your Product or Service Is Sustainable through Patents, Trademarks, First-Mover Advantage, and Continuous Improvement

Successfully launching your product or service is a great first step, but long-term success is dependent on protecting your intellectual capital with patents or trademarks, or both. Staying ahead of your competitors also means continuously improving your product or service.

4. Secure Your Product or Service's Profitability

Due to initial start-up costs, very few products or services are profitable when they're first introduced. Yet survival and success are dependent on taking in more than you pay out. Profits are for a company what a salary is to an employee.

5. Build an Effective Team

While all new products or services begin with a sole individual's idea, they seldom get off the ground without a team. That team should include both the entrepreneurial leader and team members with complementary skills.

Now, let's take our first step with a search for a problem . . . a problem whose solution will be an *opportunity.*

CHAPTER 1

Finding a Commercially Viable Problem

A Toilet Before Its Time

There will always be frustrated customers who have problems that need to be solved. As a consumer, you've probably experienced some of this frustration yourself, or at least seen it in others.

In marketing, one of the oldest sayings is, "Find a need and fill it." In other words, if you find an unsatisfied need, you'll find a problem whose solution *may* provide an opportunity for you. I've italicized the word "may," because not all problems that need to be solved are ready to be solved commercially. In other words, the demand for the product or service must be great enough to earn and sustain a profit.

An excellent example of a product that solved a "real" need at the time it was invented, but that wasn't commercially viable, was the flush toilet. Its inventor, Sir John Harrington, presented the toilet as a gift for Queen Elizabeth I of England in 1569. Certainly, Harrington was solving an important problem: the sanitary disposal of human waste.

However, his toilet wasn't commercially viable until the late 1800s. Why? Because no adequate sewer systems existed until the Industrial Age. The shifts in population from the country to cities created a demand for flush toilets in great enough numbers to establish a large and growing market.

Though Sir John's product was a bust financially, entrepreneurs like Thomas Crapper and John Douglas were so successful that their names remain linked with the flush toilet even today. Clearly, you need not be an inventor to be a successful entrepreneur. All you need is to be able to recognize a problem that is commercially viable and develop a unique solution.

Looking at Sir John's invention, you could claim Harrington was so far ahead of his time that the flush toilet didn't have a chance to be successful in the 1560s. Yet a product could be perfectly timed and still fail. I've seen numerous instances of this in my career. Take, for example, Canada Dry's Sport Cola, the first caffeine-free cola, which was introduced in 1968. At the time, I worked as a sales supervisor for a franchised Canada Dry bottler, which was based in Southern, New York. Canada Dry at that time was the third-largest soft drink brand in the world. My job was to lead the salesforce in introducing the product in our territory.

Canada Dry realized that most parents wouldn't allow their young children to drink coffee, but that they would give their children cola. The company concluded that, given a choice, parents would prefer giving their children caffeine-free cola.

The product failed miserably and cost Canada Dry millions of dollars. It wasn't that the public only wanted caffeinated drinks; the public simply wasn't aware of the caffeine problem in great enough numbers to make Sport Cola successful. Only in the seventies did health concerns over caffeine and other beverage ingredients become so great that they resulted in a change in labeling laws. Greater awareness about health issues, which was largely perpetuated by the media, created an opportunity for a whole list of food and drink products to be created: low-fat milk products, low-carbohydrate beer, and "natural" soft drinks. Entire "natural" grocery chains, such as Whole Foods, even came into being.

As we've learned, identifying a unique solution to a problem isn't always enough. Having a unique solution for a problem that's *ready* to be solved is what good entrepreneurship is all about.

Demand: How Much Is Enough?

"Is a problem *ready* to be solved?" is a convenient way of asking, "Is there enough *demand* for the product or service I'm about to create to make it commercially viable? Will there be enough demand that translates into sales volume to pay the bills and show a profit?"

In the case of the flush toilet, the answer to whether it was commercially viable is very obvious with the gift of 20/20 hindsight. But how do we make these determinations in real time when we are faced with the challenge? The answer lies in assessing the size of the market (large and growing ones are the best) and how big a chunk of the market you can chop off.

David Koffman, a successful entrepreneur who came to speak in my class, often told my students, "In niches there are riches." A niche is a portion of a market that you've identified as having some special characteristic and that's worth marketing to.[1] *Portion* is the key word in this definition, because it means settling on a segment that you can own with your solution.

Niche marketing is most practical and successful when markets reach saturation. Market saturation, according to BusinessDictionary.com, is the "point at which a market is no longer generating new demand for a firm's products, due to competition, decreased need, obsolescence, or some other factor."[2]

A classic example of how effective this strategy is can be found in the automobile industry. At its beginning, automobiles came in pretty much the same size and color. Even after sales volume grew, there was very little variety in models or even color. Production in the United States in 1923 reached 3.27 million, and the black Ford Model T accounted for just under 52 percent of the cars produced in the country.[3] One of Henry Ford's famous quotes drives this point home: "You can have any color as long as it's black."[4]

In 1920, after taking over a conglomerate of automakers that would eventually become General Motors, Pierre DuPont promptly named a brilliant young manager named Alfred Sloan to run the firm. Sloan's challenge and seemingly impossible task was to crack Ford's dominance. At the time, Ford held just over 61 percent of the car market.

The Perils of Head-to-Head Competition

It's always tempting to take the leader on head-to-head, because that's where the volume is, and where there's seemingly the most to gain. Sloan, however, quickly ruled out competing on a head-to-head pricing strategy. He realized it would take a sizeable amount of money to do so, far out of his company's reach. This is also most certainly true for the majority of people creating new products or services, and even major companies. Jay Yarrow, editor for "SAI," the tech section of *Business Insider*, told us in 2013 that since the first quarter of 2005, Microsoft's online division, Online Services Division, which is made up of Bing, MSN, and other pieces, has lost $10.9 billion.[5] As of 2014 they seem to be making headway because of their partnership with Yahoo; however, things aren't all rosy with this arrangement. Bing's "search" share of the market was up in June 2013 to 17.9 percent, while Yahoo's dropped to 11.4 percent, according to comScore. The percentage Bing grew was exactly the amount of market share Yahoo lost.[6]

Unlike Microsoft, Sloan decided to settle for a niche. Competing on engineering superiority appeared to be the most promising strategy. Charles Kettering, the legendary inventor of the electric starter and high-compression V8 engine, was the head of his engineering staff. In 1920 they were working on an air-cooled engine and planned to incorporate it into their 1923 Chevrolet to compete with the Ford's dominant Model T.

However, Sloan became impatient due to delays resulting from technical problems that he felt were disrupting his marketing plan. He ordered the development of the air-cooled engine sidetracked and instead introduced Chevrolet with nine-year-old technology. He chose a different niche—design—and relied on a new body style. He gave his mass-produced car the look of an expensive, craft-built luxury car by lowering the roof, raising the hood, and rounding the lines. Sales were brisk, convincing Sloan that it wasn't necessary to compete with Ford by leading in engineering. What was important was producing better-looking cars and giving drivers more variety. In 1923, GM sold 800,000 vehicles and earned $80 million.[7] David Koffman was right: in niches there are riches.

Small Niches Can Be Profitable

Keep in mind that all products and services serve niche markets when they start. Some go on to command large segments of the market, yet others remain small but rewarding for the companies that survive in an environment with relatively modest demand. The hand-crafted luxury car niche is an example of a niche that has remained small for many years, and yet is still highly profitable for certain companies. In 2013, Rolls-Royce announced its highest-ever annual sales, delivering 3,630 cars in its fourth consecutive record-breaking year. This made Rolls-Royce the best-selling automaker in the world of cars that cost more than $250,000.[8]

Design, the strategy that Sloan used, is the clear winner when it comes to quick results. Lexus used this strategy with its early models, which looked strikingly similar to the much more expensive Mercedes-Benz. More recently Hyundai's original design of the Genesis and current design of the Equus have had me making double-takes when they drive past me, as I mistake them for Mercedes and BMWs. We'll have to wait awhile to find out if the electric car and Tesla become the dominant segment of the car industry.

In the end, the answer to the question, "How much demand is enough?" is situational. I have always relied on a more practical question: Can I afford it? In other words, can we eventually sell enough to make a profit? Can we afford to lose money in the short term while building sales? It helps to do research to reduce uncertainty and provide some peace of mind. Yes, you can't research a product that doesn't exist, but you can research users of similar products to learn how many there are, the size of the market in dollars, and the income levels of buyers, along with other valuable demographic indicators. So how do you go about finding a problem whose solution is commercially viable?

Our search begins with *primary demand*, which is consumer interest in purchasing an entire class of products, versus consumers wanting only to purchase a certain brand within that class.[9]

Understanding Primary Demand

Several years ago I attended the Owner/President Management program at Harvard, for owners of companies with sales between $2 million and $200 million. Marty Marshall, head of the program, asked, "Is it possible to create primary demand?" What followed was a lively discussion among some of my entrepreneur classmates. They were trying very hard to make the case that "Yes, you can." Marty made several attempts to explain that no, it wasn't possible: you can't get people to do something that they're not naturally inclined to do. He went on to explain that human needs, wants, and behavior are what create demand. Surprisingly, my classmates would have no part of this, which brought on Marty's frustrated retort, "Harvard has been studying this for over 300 years, and we don't have one case where someone has actually done this. But if you want to try, that's certainly your prerogative."

My favorite primary demand question to my own classes is, "Can you sell snowballs to Inuit people?" At least one student always answers with a resounding yes. That student's favorite comeback is, "I know people who can sell anything." I then tell that student that I've never come across someone who can do this, and that it defies logic. First, this is underestimating the intelligence of the Inuit, who are experts in dealing with their environment. Second, all that the Inuit have to do to make snowballs is reach down and grab some snow.

However, asking if you could sell them gloves and boats that would make them comfortable and safe out in the cold constitutes the real primary demand question. There are plenty of variations you could provide that could potentially separate you from your competitors; for example, you could offer gloves insulated with a new material that will keep their hands warm and dry longer, or boats coated with a new protectant that will increase their life expectancy.

Once we have identified a class of products or services, then our search for a commercially viable problem becomes much clearer. A good example is the travel industry. According to the U.S. Department of Transportation, Americans flew over 575 million miles in 2011 and drove over 3.65 billion miles in passenger cars.[10]

I often tell my students that the passenger airliner is an extension of the donkey. This always gets a look of astonishment. "What we're talking about," I tell them, "is the travel industry. When people wanted to go farther then their legs would carry them, they started riding donkeys, then horses, bikes, railroads, cars, buses, and then airplanes." The desire to travel is "primary demand," and the many ways we do it is how we solve the consumer's problem of how to get this done.

I then go on to tell them about my experience in Denton, Texas, a small town near a horse-training facility where my son was interning. One day I asked a local waitress how often she got out of Denton. "Never," she said. "Why would I ever leave here, if everything I want is here?"

If everyone in America were like our waitress, there would be a very small travel industry. Fortunately for the industry, most of us love to travel, as evidenced by our history.

The Value of Being Prepared

In the previous example, entrepreneurs thinking about launching a start-up airline should know how airline travel started and how it has evolved—what's worked and what hasn't. Whenever I start a new project, I study the relevant industry to see who and what is successful and how they're doing what I'm trying to do. There's no need to "reinvent the wheel," as they say. We should learn from the successes and failures of others.

Doing your homework means being on top of what's happening today in an industry. In the broader travel industry, entrepreneurs have developed new and different, unique ways of solving our problems. For example, the Citi Bike system, operated by NYC Bike Share, features thousands of bikes at hundreds of stations around New York. Citi Bikes are available 24/7, 365 days a year. Station locations are based on population and transit needs and were selected through a participatory public input process.[11] In New York City, storage space is limited; not having to own a bike but being able to use one at your convenience (and pay a fee to do so) solves real problems for countless consumers. Zipcar, the car-sharing company, operates on a similar premise. (I recently paid $54.00 to park my car for three hours in New York City!)

As Citi Bike and Zipcar demonstrate, some of the best entrepreneurial ideas come from studying human behavior. It's my favorite place to look for a commercially viable problem.

Understanding Human Behavior: "Mother-in-Law" Research

I remember a lunch with Marty, my mentor, in the Harvard Faculty Dining Room while I was attending the Owner/President Management program. I asked him if he read *Beverage Industry* magazine. He was so on top of what was happening in our industry. "No," he said, so quickly that I thought he was going to bite my head off. "I don't, and if you need to read it to find out what's going on, you're not doing your job. It and all publications like that are six months behind what's going on."

"Well, how do you know so much about the beverage industry?" I asked.

He responded, "I watch you guys and ladies when you come to our program every year. A while back, you would look around at lunch and men would be drinking a mixed drink or a beer, never soft drinks. A short while later, all of a sudden they were drinking soft drinks but would never be caught dead drinking a diet version. Look around the tables—what do you see?"

I glanced around at the men and saw a lot of soft drinks and iced tea on the tables; many of the men were drinking diet versions of their beverage.

"What do think is driving this, your advertising?" asked Marty. "No way. It's because it's become socially unacceptable to drink alcoholic beverages during the day and at work. They're also starting to watch their waistlines and are looking for alternatives. I watch closely what all of you are doing, and I also do what I call 'mother-in-law' research. When I'm at parties or gatherings, I'm always interviewing people, asking what they drink, eat, read, watch on TV, and what they think the hot topic of the day is."

"Marty, I've been doing that for a long time too," I said. "I loved to observe people in stores and interview them about their purchases and choices." I always watched closely when companies changed their logos and product designs. Monitoring new technology and developments fascinated me.

"It's also the way we do things at Adirondack," I went on. When we called on customers, we could always check out the grocery stores afterward. After evening meetings and subsequent dinners, we would return to the grocery stores to watch and interview shoppers.

"Marty," I said, "you restored my faith in how we operate and gave me a huge boost to my self-esteem. That alone is worth the price of the program."

"Get rid of your office and get out in the trade," Marty said. "Keep doing what you do."

My favorite story about human behavior leading to a product is the Walkman. Akio Morita, cofounder and former chairman of Sony, is said to be the inspiration behind the development of the Walkman. He identified with the global hip-hop culture and loved art and music, especially opera, and he wanted to be able to listen to his favorite music on the very long flights he often took. For this to be feasible, the device would have to provide the listener with as good of an experience as a car stereo and yet be portable, allowing the user to listen to music while doing something else.

He was confident that the Walkman would be successful after observing his children and their friends, who seemed to want to play their music all day and into the night. He was also encouraged by the increasing number of people who actually took bulky stereos with them to the beach and park.

He gave his engineering team less than four months to produce the model, saying, "This is the product that will satisfy those young people who want to listen to music all day. They'll take it everywhere with them, and they won't care about record functions. If we put a playback-only headphone stereo like this on the market, it'll be a hit."[12]

Since their launch in 1979, an estimated 400 million Walkmans have been sold.

People First, Technology Second

In his book *Innovation and Entrepreneurship*, famed management theorist Peter F. Drucker makes a strong case for what he calls "social innovation"—innovation driven more by social needs than technology.[13] This is a terrific point that every aspiring entrepreneurial leader needs to take into consideration.

One interesting phenomenon I've witnessed, especially in recent years, is the "love affair with technology." It's especially prevalent with inventors, engineers, and IT specialists. So many times in my class or while working with aspiring entrepreneurs, I see these individuals dwelling exclusively on their newfound technology. Missing in every case I've encountered is a market savvy for their new discoveries.

One specific example was a student of mine, Ray Latipov, who had to make a presentation to investors that our school had brought together for the occasion. Ray was a physicist and had invented something called the Virtusphere. The Virtusphere is a hollow ten-foot sphere that's placed on a platform; the platform allows the sphere to rotate freely in any direction directed by the user's footsteps. The platform and technology are special and unique because they allow users to be immersed in an interactive virtual experience. The user's footsteps, in addition to rotating the sphere, also act as a mouse on a keyboard, allowing him or her to travel in a virtual environment and interact with other Virtusphere users.[14]

Ray's challenge was that he would only be allowed ten minutes for the presentation. It wasn't a lot of time to present a technically complicated project, one that had several patents and one whose entrepreneur was looking for several million dollars in investment. To make the effort even more difficult, Ray had only been in our country for a couple of years, and although his English was remarkably good for this short period, he struggled to present a project as complicated as this. Our dean asked me to assist him in the presentation.

Ray wanted to spend most of the ten minutes explaining his beloved technology. Fortunately I convinced him that we needed to persuade the investors that there was a market for his product. What problem would it solve? Would someone buy the product? This was the key to winning over the investors.

Unfortunately, we weren't successful in obtaining financing. However, Ray was successful in finding investors by providing them with the market potential of his remarkable technology. He went on to appear on *Shark Tank,* although once again he didn't receive funding. One of the Sharks came close to investing but backed out, stating a "too high" asking price for stock in the company. He also commented that it was the most unique technology that had been on the show up until that time.

Ray and his brother, Nurulla, who's an engineer, are currently operating Virtusphere Inc. in Binghamton, New York. Their list of customers includes Lockheed Martin, the U.S. Marine Corps, Orlando Science Center, West Point Academy, and the Air Force.

In so many of the cases above, beginning with "a toilet before its time," technology preceded an eventually profitable product or service. Later examples include the Global Positioning System, or GPS, which was first developed by the military in 1960 but formally introduced in 2000, and the Internet, which was also first developed in the 1960s but only became available to the public in the early 1990s. In each of these cases, plenty of resources, time, and emotion were invested with little or no upfront financial return.

Local Needs and Wants

Oftentimes entrepreneurs will have more luck by examining what's missing in local or regional markets. In many cases, certain products available in larger cities may not have trickled down to smaller markets.

In my hometown at the time of Scotia, New York, for example, one of my biggest pet peeves for a long time was that I couldn't find a "real" Manhattan-style bagel. Having spent a lot of time in the New York City area on business, I'd fallen in love with Manhattan-style bagels. My solution was to open a Manhattan Bagel Shoppe with my son-in-law Mike and daughter Diane right in Scotia, New York.

After months of researching the local bagel market, we opened our doors in the fall of 1989. We reached our break-even point in ninety days, which surprised even me. After five months in business, we became profitable—an amazing feat for a start-up business.

In the spirit of full disclosure, this wasn't something I could have done without having many years of experience in business and observing people. Having a great team and money to risk that I could afford to lose, with very little—if any—change to my personal living standard, was also a huge benefit.

General Needs

The cell phone is an excellent example of finding an opportunity through a general need. People have always wanted to be able to communicate away from home in a convenient manner, and the cell phone filled this need.

I remember being an early user of the car phone. I resisted it for a very long time, because one of the few places that I could get away from it all was in my car, but I finally gave way. It was a big help, because in the past I would never leave for an appointment with a customer until I had answered all my calls. This could create a problem in getting to the appointment on time. With the phone in my car, I could call on the way, which saved me a great deal of time. The same was true when returning. I remember spending three hours in a phone booth on the Massachusetts Turnpike, returning customers' calls that my secretary gave me when I called in. With my car phone, I made all these calls while driving home on the Mass Pike and the New York Thruway.

It wasn't until the late 1990s, however, that cellular phones became available to the average consumer (my initial car phone bill ran over $3,000 a month—not a big deal for a company whose revenue was $60 million, but a lot for the everyday Jane or Joe). Digital technology and cellular towers just about everywhere have made this possible. With the addition of Bluetooth technology to cell phones and cars, it also became easier and safer to talk when driving.

Customer Service

Another great place to look for opportunities is within the realm of customer service in a preexisting organization. It's the easiest need to fill, because it's something that most anyone can do. It doesn't require a great deal of education, money, or training. All that is needed is the desire and will to serve others.

I saw firsthand how an improvement in customer service could translate into a commercially viable opportunity when I took over a territory near Syracuse, New York, for Canada Dry. It was a challenging territory, since it was 40 miles from headquarters and usually required 150 miles of driving a day—oftentimes, we'd make up to 60 sales calls. To complicate matters, it was smack dab in the middle of the New York State "snow belt."

In the beverage industry at the time, it was the general practice for salespeople to make 45 to 50 in-person sales calls per day. Given their time constraints, it was easy to understand why the salespeople before me didn't spend a lot of time "filling" the shelves with soft drinks for the customer. Yet even the salesman for the local brand never spent any time filling the shelves, despite having more time on his hands than his competitors.

This was the opening I needed to create a comparative advantage over our competitor; customer service was the answer to break this market for our brand. I started filling shelves for customers, and this action quickly yielded benefits.

The major breakthrough came with one of our largest accounts, Ike's IGA. I'd struggled with this account for some time, but after I started stocking the shelves, I started to see progress as my orders grew gradually and steadily.

"Ange," said the owner, Ike, one day, "let's have a cup of coffee." *Great, I thought to myself, I need this like a hole in the head. I'll be lucky to get home by 8:00 PM.* Because Ike was a nice guy and a good customer, I said yes. I was also intrigued, because Ike said little apart from what he wanted to order.

"Ange," he said, once we'd sat down, "you come in here and work your butt off. No one before you ever did, and neither does your competitor. You're not afraid to get your hands dirty, and I appreciate what you do for me. We're going to take good care of you when you're not here."

And so began a four-year period of growth, in which our sales quadrupled. From that day on, Ike's people serviced the shelves when I wasn't there, providing a huge boost to our sales. Ike was also the first to allow me to put up large displays for promotions, eventually on a permanent basis. This was huge for us, as soft drink sales increase dramatically with off-shelf displays.

I was to carry this lesson with me to Bev-Pak. When I became the general manager, 90 percent of our sales consisted of contract packing—producing store brands and branded products for other companies. Adirondack, a brand owned by Bev-Pak, constituted the remainder of our sales. At the time, Adirondack was being sold as a control brand for local wholesalers and small independent grocers not big enough to have their own private brand.

It was obvious that we needed time to build the Adirondack brand and that we couldn't rely on a well-known brand image to create sales. Our answer was customer service: we could out-service our competitors. It started with the phone: our people would answer each call by the second ring and, after announcing our name, would give the caller their name. Customers weren't allowed to be put on hold for more than 20 seconds (a beeper would go off on the phone when it reached this time point).

At the same time, we initiated a 100 percent guarantee that we'd provide service, as long as we had three days' notice. Our competitors with the same distribution system as ours required a one-week notice. Customer service was vital in building Bev-Pak and eventually Adirondack. The company is still known to this day as having outstanding customer service not rivaled by competitors, and they still answer the phone by the second ring.

Timing and Strategy

Timing is the crucial factor in making a strategy successful. In their book *Marketing Warfare*, Al Ries and Jack Trout tell us that timing and strategy are the "Himalayas"; everything else is the "Catskills."[15] As we've discussed, strategy is a goal accompanied by a plan to achieve it. Timing, as I define it, is "doing the right thing at the right time."

A great example of excellent timing is Hamdi Ulukaya, the founder of Chobani Inc., whose story is similar to mine. In 1994 Ulukaya, a Turkish immigrant, moved from New York City to Albany, New York, where he started attending classes at Albany University while working on a farm to support himself.

In 2004, Ulukaya saw an ad for a Kraft yogurt plant that was for sale. He visited the plant and found that it was run down, with old equipment. Nevertheless, with the help of a small business loan, he bought it for an undisclosed amount and soon was ready to produce his own yogurt.

Ulukaya's background meant he was very familiar with yogurt, an ancient food that he enjoyed growing up. He remembered that in Europe and Asia, consumers were accustomed to Greek yogurt that they knew was "strained," a process that removed much of the liquid whey, lactose, and sugar. So why not Greek yogurt in America? Yogurt that was thicker and creamier, that Ulukaya was convinced tasted better than the American version, would have a comparative advantage. Another advantage would be its perception of being healthier: in the same amount of calories as regular yogurt, Greek yogurt doubled the amount of protein and reduced the amount of sugar by half.

Mr. Ulukaya, I'm sure, did his homework, recognizing that there was a serious problem that needed to be solved in America—23.9 million children ages two to nineteen were overweight; of these children, 12.7 million were obese. Among American adults, more than 78 million were obese.[16] This indeed was a problem *ready* to be solved. According to a 2014 USDA study, working-age adults were making earnest efforts to cut back on the number of calories they consumed, and to eat more meals at home.[17]

Convinced that the timing was perfect for both Greek yogurt and its "straining" process to be introduced in America, the question was: Would it be difficult to acquire this technology? Hardly—it's been around commercially for a very long time. Fage (pronounced "fa-yeh") began producing Greek yogurt in 1926, selling it to retail outlets that sold it in bulk. In 1975 Fage began a branding concept in Greece, selling their product in smaller sealed tubs with attractive packaging similar to what they use today. In 1988 they started exporting their product to the United Kingdom; it reached our shores in 1998.[18]

Mr. Ulukaya's timing has proven to be very rewarding: by the end of 2014, Chobani's sales were projected to reach $1 billion.

The Best-Case Scenario: When Strategy Meets Technology

As Mr. Ulukaya will tell you, this intersection can be a windfall for the entrepreneurial leader. What I'm also sure he'd tell you is that there's no magic formula as to when the timing is right. The trick is in knowing and studying history, human behavior, and your environment.

Conversely, entrepreneurial leaders always have to be on the lookout for a "negative" convergence of timing and a need being met. In the late eighties, a friend of mine who owned a video store told me he was concerned about movies being available through cable. "Ange," he said, "it's just a matter of time before our stores will be out of business. I'm going to make as much money as I can and invest it somewhere else before this happens." My friend nailed this: Netflix's business model took awhile to catch on, but once it did, it decimated "physical" video stores like Blockbuster, which closed all its stores on January 11, 2014.

A few months ago, Apple made it so that another friend's prediction thirty years ago finally came true: people are talking into their watches. As they say, the world is a-changing, which leads us to our next area to search: change.

Changes = Opportunity

Change is perhaps the most "constant" place to seek a commercially viable opportunity. Through my own experience and academic research, I've found that certain changes tend to yield more entrepreneurial opportunities than most. They include demographic changes, societal "changes in perception," and "disruptive" changes, including new technologies and worldwide areas of instability.

Demographic Changes

Demographic shifts in our population can create significant problems for society and tremendous opportunities for entrepreneurs. The aging U.S. population, for example, is creating many opportunities for entrepreneurs in the health-care market. The federal government provided $40 billion in incentives for health-care providers to convert to meaningful electronic records. Companies assisting in this transition have found a great deal of new business.

Changes in Perception

Closely related to demographic shifts are changes in perception. One only has to watch the morning TV news shows to see how a change in perception has impacted a whole industry. Until recently, women weren't seen as credible hosts of morning shows or network nightly news programs.

There also weren't a heck of lot of women entrepreneurs, and now we have a host of them, including the incredible Oprah.

Changes Resulting from National and Worldwide Instability

On a macro level, unexpected change that's causing a serious problem for the general public can be an excellent way to capitalize on an entrepreneurial opportunity. Ideally, this should be a change that's receiving a great deal of publicity.

In 1973, the Arab members of OPEC—the Organization of the Petroleum Exporting Countries—decided to impose an embargo on U.S. oil. Oil prices doubled and then quadrupled, imposing skyrocketing costs on consumers and challenging the stability of our national economy. The government introduced "emergency" measures, including the creation of the Strategic Petroleum Reserve, a national 55-mile-per-hour speed limit on U.S. highways, and later, fuel economy standards during the Ford administration.

You'd think the "Big Three"—GM, Ford, and Chrysler—would have capitalized on the opportunity to create small, fuel-efficient cars. Instead, they maintained the status quo with large, more expensive gas-guzzlers. Meanwhile, Japanese automakers like Honda, Toyota, and Nissan crept up on U.S. automakers, commanding 22.4 percent of the U.S. auto market by 1988, versus just 6.1 percent of the market in 1973. By 1990 U.S. automakers had lost close to $30 billion.[19, 20, 21]

While unexpected change can yield big opportunities, it's important to remember that not all dramatic and highly publicized events represent good ways to generate new business. In fact, they can have the opposite effect.

Take the 2000 Florida election debacle. Originally, tiny bits of paper called "hanging chad" made reading votes very difficult, and in some cases, impossible. As a result of this, from 2003 to 2005, some $3 billion flew out of federal coffers to fund "new" versions of voting equipment. Nothing said "cutting-edge" and "state of the art" more than electronic voting machines. One of them, the AccuVote, made by Diebold Election Systems, became the market leader by a sizable margin.

The euphoria over this unbelievably fast-growing market subsided when these machines ran into problems. According to a 2004 *Bloomberg News* article, computer security experts at Johns Hopkins and Rice universities said the machines were vulnerable to vote rigging. Parts of California and Ohio even banned the use of the machines, due to security concerns and operating flaws. In 2006 Diebold, whose main business is automated teller machines (ATMs), sold the voting-machine unit to another company for $5 million—about one-fifth of what the federal government paid in 2002.[22]

There's no question that the problem with voting machines in our country needs to be solved. However, this may be a classic example of a problem that is not *ready* to be solved. Or, more specifically, we have not found the "right" (commercially viable) solution to the problem. It is also another way of saying that the problem doesn't exist to the point where it could be solved.

Solving Problems That Don't Exist

In searching for a commercially viable opportunity, beware of trying to "solve" a "problem" that doesn't necessarily need solving. In 1985, Coca-Cola announced that they were changing their original formula and introducing "New Coke" instead. Almost immediately, consumers expressed their outrage. After only 79 days Coca-Cola brought back the old formula, which the company rebranded as "Coca-Cola Classic." In just two days after the announcement of Coca-Cola Classic, the company received 31,600 hotline calls reassuring them that they'd made the right decision. This should have been all the proof Coke needed to understand that there never was a problem.

The Haves Resist Change

It's important to remember that the "haves," or market leaders, often resist change. In fact, they often ignore or refuse to recognize change in the market, including their own status, often with severe consequences. Sears, for example, "wouldn't admit for the longest time that Wal-Mart and Kmart were their real competition," according to Sam Walton, in his biography, *Made in America*.[23] Walton goes on to say that Sears "ignored both of us, and we both flew right by them."

I had a similar experience during the first turnaround I led at Bev-Pak. A representative from our largest customer at the time, Grand Union, a leading grocer in the Northeast, came to me with a problem. "Ange, my bottle supplier won't make 48-ounce soft drinks for us in our store brand," he said. I didn't bother to ask him why, because I knew the answer. Our competitor supplied this customer with their bottle beverages (a 28-ounce size at the time), and we supplied them with cans. The competitor, who as a "have"—the leader in providing store-brand soft drinks—rightly believed that a 48-ounce size would cut into the sales of the 28-ounce size. The competitor knew that the 48-ounce size was a better value.

At the time, given our status as a "have-not," we had minimal capacity to manufacture bottles—certainly not this new size, which would require a major change in production. I had to convince the owner of our company to make an investment of $20,000—no small task at the time, since we were under a very tight budget.

Fortunately we listened to our customer and seized an opportunity. The benefits to us were significant. Not only were the sales of the store brand substantial, but also our new production capabilities made it possible to produce our own 48-ounce beverages. Within a year, sales of the 48-ounce size had netted nearly $10 million, with Adirondack leading the way. In the words of Sam Walton, we "flew past" our competitor, who began a sales volume slide that led to bankruptcy just a few years later.

Disruption

The concept of "disruptive" technology certainly isn't new in the field of entrepreneurship. In his 1942 book *Capitalism, Socialism, and Democracy,* the great economist Joseph A. Schumpeter wrote,

> Innovation by the entrepreneur leads to gales of creative destruction as innovations cause old inventories, ideas, technologies, skills, and equipment to become obsolete.[24]

Even if you're the market leader, "attacking yourself before your competitors do"—a concept outlined in Ries and Trout's classic book, *Marketing Warfare*—is an excellent defensive strategy.[25] It's advice I'm sure my competitor wished it had followed. Introducing new products, or better versions of existing products and services, even if you're the market leader, will beat your competition to the punch.

Oftentimes market leaders are the most skittish when it comes to attacking themselves—an ironic fact, since they have the most to lose. One only needs to look to Kodak for a sad example of this. In 1975, Kodak invented the technology we use in every brand of smartphone and digital camera. Yet they refused to market it, for fear that they would jeopardize their traditional products, which at one time commanded 90 percent of the U.S. film market. The result? Between 2002 and 2012, Kodak lost 87 percent of its business, and in 2012 it declared bankruptcy.[26]

"Never Buy a Business You Don't Understand"

My first business mentor, Carl Touhey, the owner and CEO of a company I'd once worked for, cautioned me, "Ange, never buy a business that you don't understand, because you'll go broke before you learn it." Over the years, I've learned the truth of Carl's words: it is in fact business suicide to buy a business whose user you don't understand.

I learned this lesson up close and personal while working as a Canada Dry salesman in the early 1960s. Our flavored soft drink can sales were not what they should have been—a result, I believed, of a failure to emotionally engage the consumer with our designs. The cans, as they were, were just solid colors—orange for orange soda, dark blue for grape—with the company's logo on the front. Canada Dry decided to take a risk and redesign the cans, replacing the logo with vignettes of fruits. Our sales increased by 400 percent as a result. I had no market research to explain why this happened; what I knew is that the beautiful pictures of fruits on the cans sure made them appealing. It brought to mind a lesson I learned with a flip chart that they gave us to help sell our products. One of the frames showed food mixed all together—it was a real mess. On the next frame in the chart was a picture of the same food, separated into nice, neat piles, in a much better-looking image. The point was that food is more appealing when presented properly. I figured this was certainly the case with soft drinks, and seeing it was enough to know that it certainly worked.

I kept this experience in mind many years later, after I'd become the sales manager at Bev-Pak (the name of our company before we changed it to Adirondack Beverages). My first "assignment" was to redesign our product line. I placed vignettes on all of our flavored products, and our sales increased dramatically. I'll never forget when an out-of-state driver picked up merchandise at our plant and asked to buy our grape soft drink because he couldn't buy it in his area. Before the design change, we couldn't sell our products very well in his market—or, for that matter, in any of the markets we were in. We had limited distribution, making it difficult for customers to find our products. And where we did offer our products, sales weren't very good.

However, our most effective and rewarding design innovation came in 1984, when we introduced the soft drink industry's first proprietary plastic bottle. When plastic was first introduced in the late 1970s, the beverage industry had adopted a universal generic bottle for all sizes of soft drinks. The result was that all brands and private-label bottles looked exactly alike—the only difference being the label. Use of this generic plastic bottle remained the standard practice for several years.

I realized, from my experience as a Canada Dry salesman, that there was an opportunity for my company to gain significant market share. I thought that we could accomplish this with an attractive "special," proprietarily designed bottle. Knowing that the average grocery store consumer spends half a second looking at items on a shelf, I thought that we'd benefit tremendously from having an attractive product, one that really stood out. Designing such an attractive bottle would also unquestionably improve the customer's perception of the quality of our drinks.

I also had a good feeling about our proprietary design, based on Coke's success with its six-ounce light-green glass bottle, which it introduced in 1916. The bottle was certainly the most recognized—and I should add admired—product in the world, amazingly without a label. At the time, Coke introduced the curved green bottle because its bottlers worried that a straight-sided bottle wasn't distinctive enough; consumers could easily confuse Coca-Cola with other brands. Unbelievably, Coke gave up the goodwill earned by this image when it started using the industry-wide generic plastic bottle in 1978.[27]

The product we chose to introduce in our "special" bottle was our one-liter seltzer water. Seltzer water appealed to a segment of the market that was viewed as "ethnic" (people of European descent), as well as to native-born New Yorkers. Even though the market for seltzer water was quite large, it was difficult to make a profit: there was very little brand recognition, and sales were being driven by "the lowest" price. Still, we saw an opportunity: along with changing our bottle design, we added natural flavors, including lemon-lime and citrus.

Our award-winning design and natural flavors increased our sales by 700 percent, or 18 million bottles annually. It did something even more valuable, in that it changed the image and perception of the product and our brand. The product was now included in the "sparkling water" category. Before, the grocery industry reporting systems hadn't included seltzer water in this segment. I doubt that many consumers did either, despite the fact that the only difference between sparkling and seltzer water is that seltzer has slightly more carbonation.

Adirondack 1-Seltzer became the leader in the Boston market in the sparkling water category within 90 days, with a 32 percent share of the supermarket distribution segment. We even surpassed well-established Perrier and Poland Springs, both of whom had been in the sparkling water market for years. Most rewarding, our product became profitable. It went from being a loser to being a significant profit contributor to our line of soft drinks.

How Much Do I Need to Know?

After reading through these examples, you might wonder if you have to be business-savvy or a marketing expert in order to find a commercially viable problem to solve. The answer is a resounding no.

To prove this point, let's take a look at how wheels ended up on luggage. Although wheels have been around for thousands of years, they didn't appear on luggage in their current form until 1987, when a Northwest Airlines pilot named Bob Plath tired of lugging his heavy overnight bag and flight bag through airports around the world. Being a creative kind of guy, Plath spent weekends working on a wheeled "pilot" bag in his garage.

The result of his efforts was to attach two wheels and a long handle to a suitcase that rolled upright. Mr. Plath initially sold his creations to his fellow crewmembers. But when everyday travelers saw flight attendants striding easily through airports with their "Rollaboards" in tow, a new way to carry luggage was created.

The most intriguing part of this story is that Bob Plath wasn't the first person to put wheels on luggage and patent this innovation. Mr. Bernard D. Sadow, a vice president at a Massachusetts company that made luggage and coats, is credited with inventing rolling luggage in 1970.

So why did it take so long for wheeled luggage to become popular? Mr. Sadow tells us he met with strong resistance on those early sales calls, when he was frequently told that men would not accept suitcases with wheels. "It was a very macho thing," he said. Unlike Plath's design, which created a telescoping handle on luggage with two wheels, Sadow's put a strap on the front of luggage, which lay horizontal on four wheels.[28]

An excellent question is why Mr. Plath and Mr. Sadow took two different approaches to solving the same problem. The answer lies in understanding the user, since these gentlemen were different types of travelers. Mr. Sadow was a business and pleasure traveler who would most often have large luggage, which he'd place on a large cart that you could rent at the airport for a dollar. If you had too many bags for a cart, porters were available to move your luggage on horizontal carts with four wheels and a handle. Mr. Plath, on the other hand, being a pilot, traveled with a smaller bag that would be placed in the carry-on compartment.

Placing a handle on the bag and adding wheels would eliminate carrying it. Adding both to larger luggage also made sense to him.

Mr. Plath's understanding of the user was a very good reason why he was successful. His company, Travelpro, enjoyed first-year sales around $1.5 million. Within a few years, Mr. Plath left the flying to others and held fifteen patents on a diverse line of rolling luggage.[29] By 2003 Travelpro's annual sales reached $45 million.[30]

Plath's story proves that to develop successful products, you don't need a great deal of money, a whole lot of formal education, or to be an expert in the industry you are joining. Another good example is the clothing company L. L. Bean, founded by Leon Leonwood Bean, an avid sportsman who loved to hunt and fish. Bean grew tired of having cold, wet feet in the field, so he made a pair of sturdy rubber boots. When friends and strangers saw the boots, they asked if they could buy a pair. One hundred and two years later, in 2012, the company netted $1.52 billion in sales.[31]

Making Something Out of Nothing Is "Special"

Mr. Plath and L. L. Bean were successful by making existing products better with new technology and materials. Creating products and services with large budgets and organizations is fine and beneficial, but creating something with scarce resources and no special technology is considerably more difficult—and special, in an entrepreneurial sense.

This is what David ("Dave") Maione, CEO of Night Shift, a commercial cleaning company, managed to do with the help of his brother and partner, Anthony ("Tony"). Twice a year Dave comes to my class to share his incredible story.

When Dave was 15 and his brother 19, they took their mother's mop, bucket, and cleaning materials and headed out to a local bank whose manager they'd convinced to give them his cleaning contract. This was the beginning of their cleaning business in Endicott, New York, which has since blossomed into the largest and most dominant cleaning company in our area. Their customers include Security Mutual Life Insurance Company, Columbian Financial Group, and Willow Run Foods. Dave always tells my class that the managers of local businesses wanted to help "these two young guys who were aspiring entrepreneurs." He also tells them how his brother wouldn't let him out of the business arrangement when he attended Cornell University. While Dave was earning his bachelor's degree, he drove back and forth from Endicott to Ithaca, New York, every day—a distance of fifty-five miles each way—to be able to keep his end of the bargain.

In 1995 Tony came up with the idea to start a second business, Core Management Services, a cleaning consulting company. Tony is now the CEO of Core Management, which now serves major corporations in the United States and Europe such as Corning, Pfizer, Merck, and Phillips 66. Their clients also include major universities, such as New York University, the University of Vermont, and Harvard University.

Another thing that Dave likes to tell my students is that Night Shift isn't a very sophisticated company. This always gets a chuckle out of me, as I have to tell my students that they've created proprietary software and the most sophisticated program available to provide cleaning services for buildings and facilities of all sizes, shapes, and forms. These services are responsible for their huge client list of very well-known and prominent organizations.

What I love about what Dave and Tony did is that they took a problem that most people truly dislike (dirt and cleaning) and turned it into two businesses with annual multimillion-dollar revenues. They did this with no money, no formal education, and no powerful friends. Now *that's* making something special out of nothing!

Closing Thoughts: Ideas versus Opportunities

Are all ideas opportunities? Considering that the average person has 70,000 thoughts per day, most are definitely not.[32] It goes without saying that not all ideas are opportunities.

How can I tell the difference between an idea and an opportunity? First, let me give you an example. I have an idea for an electric car that would be able to travel 500 miles per battery charge. Is this a good idea? You bet! Is it a good opportunity? Not for me, since I have no expertise in this area. I also have no access to an organization capable of turning this idea into an opportunity.

On the other hand, it's an excellent opportunity for Tesla Motors and its founder, Elon Musk. Tesla already has a car with a 300-mile range per battery charge, terrific patented battery technology, and a talented product development department. Its main challenge might be its competitor, the Israel-based car company Phinergy, which hopes to have a car that will have a range of 1,000 miles by 2017.

A Final Word on Funding

As you move forward with pursuing your opportunity, you'll want to think about funding. If you're like the great majority of entrepreneurs, you'll probably be reaching toward your own pocket. According to a recent study funded by the Ewing Marion Kauffman Foundation, nearly 70 percent of entrepreneurs rely on their personal savings. About a quarter of entrepreneurs rely on venture capital and "angel" or private investors, while only 15 percent rely on friends and family. An even smaller percentage—about 7 percent—received funding through corporate investments.[33] Crowdfunding is also becoming a popular alternative. According to Fundable, a small-business crowdfunding platform, crowdfunding raised $5.1 billion in capital in 2012.[34]

Yet these aren't the only available funding methods, and as an entrepreneurial leader, you'll often have to think outside the box. If you live in the United States, you'll definitely want to determine if your state has a program in place to help local entrepreneurs. I was fortunate enough to receive assistance in funding from the New York State Industrial Development Agency (IDA). The IDA issued double tax-free bonds—the income earned from the bond interest exempted the purchaser from both New York State and federal income taxes. This in turn resulted in a much lower interest rate (in our case a reduction of 3 percent). Contact your state, and you may find a program like the one in New York State, the IDA, which was very helpful in obtaining our funding.

If you own a small, manufacturing-based business, your suppliers might also be a source of funding, particularly when it comes to funding equipment purchases. At Adirondack, our can and equipment supplier, Crown Cork & Seal, purchased the IDA bonds, funding our purchase and supplying us with working capital.

Finally, if you're looking to purchase an existing business, quite often the seller is willing to fund at least a portion of the sale with a mortgage. I've seen this many times in the restaurant business and with other small businesses.

In the end, never believe that it's impossible to get funding: where there is a will, there is always a way. My story should be all the proof you need to know this is true.

CHAPTER 2

Establishing a Comparative and Competitive Advantage

When someone comes to me for help, the first question I ask is, "What makes your business special—what's your 'hook'? In other words, what do you compete on?" If the person can't answer this question, then he isn't on top of his business. The next thing I ask is for him to tell me what they think they are, what they would like to be, and their plan to get there, in writing, on one page.

Surprisingly few entrepreneurs have a good handle on these issues—issues that are critical to establishing comparative and competitive advantages. In my own case, Harvard's Marty Marshall helped me to sharpen my focus and know where to start. Marty's advice helped Adirondack become the company it is today.

What Business Am I In?

This is a great question for all entrepreneurial leaders to ask themselves, and it's one that Marty forced us to deal with on the first day of his class. He started by telling us, "You have a tent card folded in two in front of you with your name on it. Below your name I want you to put down what business you're in. Don't tell me things like 'travel industry' or 'marketing'—and Angelo, don't put down 'sugared water' (he liked to bust on me). I want to know what businesses you're really in. I'm going to also tell you that 80 percent of you won't figure it out by the end of our program three years from now."

It took me awhile to understand what he was looking for, but with the help of his marketing classes, I got it. He wanted to learn if we knew the underlying factors that drove our businesses and "what" we were.

Our business was soft drinks, but we did more than this: we provided value to our customers. We did this with an established policy of never doing anything that wasn't as good as the major brands, and always striving to be better than them.

We also sensed the wave of concern over health issues and a potential for what we called "good-for-you" foods, an issue our competitors paid little attention to. We started upgrading our product line with all-natural flavors and not adding caffeine to our cola. In 1983, sensing that the consumer was starting to move away from sugared products, we introduced our seltzer line, Adirondack water in gallon bottles, and our diet line, Waist Watchers. Our outstanding, award-winning packaging put the finishing touches on our product line. Within two years, these two lines amounted to $11 million in annual sales.

A key part of our "value" focus was our distribution system: the supermarkets would literally distribute our product for us, utilizing their 18-wheelers and labor. This resulted in a significant cost savings to us, as well as a lot of hassle, since we didn't have to deliver our product to hundreds of individual stores. As is the case now, that system wasn't available to the larger brands, because of legal and policy restrictions. Our customers also benefited from using the system, earning revenue for providing this service.

Our pricing strategy was the final piece to the puzzle of value creation. Rather than pocket our savings to add to our profits, we passed them on to the consumer with a stay-low pricing strategy. For example, our two-liter bottles were pre-priced at 89 cents, with occasional features of 69 or 79 cents. Most important was placing a pricing sticker on the bottle during production. We knew that pricing on grocery store shelves could be difficult for consumers to understand, so we knew the sticker was a clincher.

On the other hand, the leading brands employed a "discounting" strategy, with high retail prices and heavily discounted sale prices. For example, Coke's and Pepsi's regular retail price for two-liter bottles was $1.39 each. They'd promote their products at 99 cents each, a price that would increase sales dramatically. The problem was that if consumers liked this price, they'd have to search to find the store with the sale price, and then most often they would buy their groceries there. Or consumers could wait until it was on sale and stock up on it then. The brands loved the second option because beverages are an impulse item.

Our strategy worked because we knew what we were and the business we were in: the value, satisfaction, and recognition business. We knew that in many households, when a spouse brought home a branded soft drink, his or her partner often complained that the drinks were expensive, especially if purchased at full price. In households with children, the children weren't very happy when their parents brought home an inexpensive drink. Along came Adirondack, a brand advertised on TV like the major brands—a quality beverage at an attractive and affordable price that you didn't have to work very hard to find. Bingo—the spouse and children were happy and satisfied, and the buyer received credit for being a wise shopper. Are there any parents who don't want to please their children? Is there any one of us who doesn't appreciate recognition?

Deep down in my heart, I knew we were in the soft drink business, but Marty would never let me live it down if I put that on my card. He forced me to dig down to realize just how we were keeping and growing our business, and what we were.

Later on, Joe Morone, at the time the dean of the business school at Rensselaer Polytechnic Institute (RPI), asked me to make a presentation to his MBA class about our brands and our company. Unbeknownst to me, his students did a marketing study on us and were prepared for me when I showed up. In my presentation I pretty much told them what I had learned in Marty's class about what we were and how we did it. I was amazed and gratified when they told me what they had found.

"You are absolutely right about your pricing strategy," one of the students said. "Your customers love the fact that you have everyday value pricing. They told us they didn't have to chase around to find it, and, most importantly, they could depend on it. They think the quality of your brands is outstanding. We didn't hear a single complaint, and there were raves about your products."

Later, in one of Adirondack's focus groups, one woman remarked, "I stopped bringing home the branded products. I started buying Adirondack, and my family loves it, and no one complains. There are times when I can buy the brands on sale sometimes at a price very close or even less than Adirondack. I don't do it, because I don't want to have to switch back and forth and never get them used to one thing."

What Marty did for me was to help me learn that it all boils down to two things: what you are and how you do it. I am astonished at how most people and companies defined themselves by *how* they do things rather than what they really are.

Comparative Advantage: From Ordinary to Extraordinary

Now that you know what business you're in, you must research the market you're entering into, which includes the competitors and their products and services. Working to develop a comparative advantage forces you to do your homework. When you're doing your research, it's essential that you learn what features your competitors' products or services have, and how to make your own product or service unique and better. Investors demand a strong competitive advantage—that is, proof that you can offer a better or more unique product than your competitors—before parting with their funds.

A word about the difference between a comparative advantage and a competitive advantage. I had always used the latter term, which is much more popular, until one night I saw a leading economist use the term "comparative advantage" on PBS's *Charlie Rose*. It struck me that this term forces the entrepreneurial leader to highlight the uniqueness of the strived-for advantage. In the end, however, they are both the same concept and what attracts investors and is demanded by them for just cause.

The stronger the competitive advantage, the larger premium a company can charge for its product or service. Apple, BMW, Mercedes, and Starbucks are all examples of companies that have a strong competitive advantage, which in turn affords them the opportunity to charge more for their products.

Bob Plath is a terrific example of how a comparative advantage resulted in strong competitive advantage. He didn't come up with the original idea; he merely improved on it.

Generally speaking, successful new products and services are improvements on existing technology, products, and services. For example, new environmentally friendly lightbulbs last much longer than standard lightbulbs. Hybrid cars are more energy efficient than "traditional" cars. Shatterproof windows are more durable than standard glass windows and also offer a better value, due to their high quality. The iPod has many more features than Walkmans did, and it is considered "cool"-looking. All these examples include products that were already available to the consumer, just in a different form.

Remember that although new successful products are generally improvements on existing ones, to create a strong comparative and competitive advantage, you always need to create a "wow" with the consumer. Cases in point: the iPod, the iPhone, and the Tesla Model S. Generally speaking, when customers recognize a "wow," that "wow" becomes a powerful marketing tool for your company.

Planning a Prototype

Once you've established both a comparative and a competitive advantage, developing a prototype, or "proof of concept," is a must. Your solution isn't real unless you have a prototype! Without proof that you've developed your concept, your idea is just that—an idea.

Your prototype doesn't have to be the finished product. In the auto industry, for example, a "concept car" is usually an advanced example of what the car will eventually look like. Most often, it's changed slightly before being introduced to the market. If your entrepreneurial opportunity is a service, your prototype can simply be an outline of the structure of the service, along with a management and personnel chart.

In the beverage industry, prototypes are fairly simple to produce and far less costly than in other industries. Oftentimes we'd manufacture a small batch of a product, handwrite labels, and have the customer perform a taste test. Packaging the sample was somewhat more difficult but would always produce a "wow." Several times we had a plastic bottle produced for us that would be an exact replica of the new and unique bottle we'd designed. The customer very seldom required a taste test and relied on our expertise and past performance.

Positioning a Product or Service

Just as crucial as planning a prototype is *positioning* a product or service. The term "positioning" was coined by Al Ries and Jack Trout in 1972 and refers to how a prospect holds your product or service in his or her mind.[1] It is what you want your customers to think of when they hear your product or service's name. Most people think of a "market" as being where you sell your product—whether it is local, regional, national, or international. But the real market, as Ries informs us, is the six inches between potential customers' ears.

When we first positioned Adirondack Beverages under my leadership, we had to decide what our strengths were. We knew that we had a pricing advantage over our competitors. However, price alone wasn't enough to establish the overall value that we defined as quality, service, and attractive pricing. Our goal was to be the "best value in the soft drink section," and this is what we wanted consumers to think of when they heard the name Adirondack.

An important part of positioning is creating awareness; at the time, TV and radio were the best vehicles to achieve this. In our industry, TV was required for "authorization" of your products, or the grocer agreeing to sell them. With no choice, we advertised, but with a very limited budget.

I found the reaction of the consumer very interesting. All of a sudden, we had credibility. Before our advertising on TV, few people would tell me that they had even heard of our product, let alone bought it, even though we were somehow selling several million containers at the time. Now it seemed like everyone knew who we were.

Creating awareness using advertising is always a challenge for new and start-up companies and brands, even though it appears to be easier today with social media. Certain options available to us worked then and still do. The first is using the media: stories are more valuable and more effective then paid advertising. If your company is on the news and they're touting your product, the viewer knows that it is a "real" story and not a paid-for message. The best news of all is that this kind of advertising is free.

Despite our limited TV budget, we managed to attract the local media. One day I got a phone call from Jack Arneckie, news anchor on Channel 6, our local CBS affiliate. Jack was doing a story on the soft drink industry and needed to interview an "expert." As a result of the interview, he became interested in our company and our customer and employee philosophy. Jack came in and did a story on Adirondack Beverages, focusing on our progressive leadership and our method of interacting with consumers. Afterward he'd call me any time he needed someone from the beverage industry or business in general.

Out of later stories about our company came a request from a regional (New York State and the areas surrounding New York City) 30-minute version of *60 Minutes*. They came in and did a five-minute piece entitled "The Rules of the Sandbox," about our employee programs and products. The theme of the piece was "Everything I learned about dealing with people, I learned in a sandbox."

In addition to all this, we were featured in the local newspaper and in a national trade magazine. Interestingly, I got more of reaction from the longer print articles than the quick spots on TV. I'm sure it's because the stories were more comprehensive.

Another method we used was grocers' advertising. Often grocers run promotions, including TV campaigns. The fee that they charged for these campaigns was considerably less than standard TV rates, so we often used this method, continuing on with it until we sold the company.

When we'd grown to the stage where we could afford an extensive advertising budget, we created a strategy for positioning our product. It was tempting to advertise our price, but fortunately we realized that this was a given. The consumer would see our price when he or she read a grocer's ad or went shopping and saw our pre-priced products. I expressed some concerns I had about our low prices affecting our image, to Marty.

"Do you think we have a problem with our price being consistently lower than the brands?" I asked.

"Have you ever received customer complaints about your price?" he asked.

"No way," I said. "They love the price."

"Then stop worrying about problems that don't exist," he said. I loved that response.

We decided instead to focus on establishing an image of quality in order for the consumer to believe our product was a good value. We knew that when people thought of the Adirondack Mountains and the surrounding region, the first thing that came to their minds was fresh, pure air and water, and beautiful mountains. We wanted our customers, when they thought of Adirondack soft drinks, to picture "pure, natural, and refreshing," like the air in the mountains.

Fortunately, we had a terrific water source that we also owned. The precious Adirondack Aquifer was created thousands of years ago when ice age glaciers shaped the huge underground reservoirs that hold and protect these pure, cold (53-degree), crystalline-clear waters. It helped too that the source of our water was the streams in the Adirondacks.

Since water is over 86 percent of any soft drink, it's obviously a very important ingredient. Our water is among the purest in the world. Adirondack is one of the few soft drinks you can buy that is not made with municipal water. Our water was naturally pure and naturally sodium-free, and we were going to tell people about it.

To strengthen our position of "pure" and "natural," in 1990 we introduced Clear 'n' Natural Soft Drinks, an all-natural soft drink in a proprietarily designed plastic 48-ounce bottle. It directly competed with the market leader, which sold a 28-ounce glass bottle at the same price. Our first-year sales were $5.25 million.

Selecting a Distribution System

After positioning a product or service, the next most important task for the entrepreneurial leader is selecting a distribution system. A unique distribution system can provide cost benefits and further enhance a company's competitive advantage.

Companies with large budgets can access traditional systems, including retail outlets, distributors, and franchises. Other companies, however—including your own venture—will often find themselves coming up with their own distribution system.

Adirondack used a distribution system that wasn't available to the leading brands when they were first started—the supermarket distribution system. For legal purposes, Coca-Cola and Pepsi couldn't distribute to supermarket warehouses, since they had binding agreements with franchised bottlers all around the world. The old "franchise bottler" system meant that soft drinks were delivered to individual stores literally one case at a time. Trucks had to be hand-loaded by crews, usually at night, so that they would be ready for delivery early in the morning.

We, on the other hand, used forklifts to load 100-case pallets onto 18-wheeler trucks. A truck containing 2,200 cases could be loaded in twenty minutes, whereas a crew of eight to ten people would require four hours to accomplish this. To save on delivery fees, customers themselves often swung by to pick up truckloads of soft drinks. (Amazingly, 60 percent of our sales were picked up at our location). The supermarkets would then distribute our products with their vehicles and sell our product at their stores.

Despite the efficiency of the supermarket system, direct store delivery (DSD) is still used by most beverage companies, along with many other kinds of food companies, including those providing bread and baked goods, snacks, and produce. DSD constitutes nearly a quarter—24 percent—of the total dollar sales in the grocery industry.[2]

Adirondack wasn't the first brand to utilize this system, but for us, it was a major factor in our brand's success. We saved a significant amount from not paying franchise fees and from having our own water source. That being said, no distribution system is perfect. The grocer's system provided an excellent value to our consumers and to us, while the DSD system provided more service to the grocer.

Creating Awareness

Once an entrepreneurial leader has established a sound distribution system, creating awareness—whether by TV, newspapers, magazines, the Internet, or other avenues such as word of mouth—is the next logical step. At Adirondack, we knew that the grocery store shopper was our typical customer, so we would advertise on the local news, which at that time was heavily viewed by our customers. Other programs, some of which aired in prime-time slots, were also popular with our audience: *Wheel of Fortune, Jeopardy*, and *Laugh-In*, to name a few.

Competing on Value, Not Price

Should you wish to undercut your competitors, keep in mind that the market leader can always lower its price. Companies in this position are usually financially very sound.

However, there are ways to compete on *value*, which is not the same as competing on price. Value is an assessment of the worth of a good or service. Consumers rely on "perceived value," an internal feeling about how much certain products are worth to them. For the most part, consumers are unaware of the true cost of production for the products they buy.[3]

Adirondack is the best example that I can provide regarding competing on value. Our products were produced from an outstanding water source with natural flavors, attractive design, and exceptional service at an attractive and affordable price. Adirondack exceeded our customers' expectations; they were getting the quality they expected from a national brand at a much lower price.

Competing on price is strictly being the cheapest. Very few consumers are "true price" shoppers. At a marketing seminar I once attended, we were asked if we were "price" shoppers. All of us raised our hands. The instructor then asked how many of us bought our clothes at secondhand outlets, and all the hands came down. I walked out of there convinced that competing on value is the foundation of sustaining a brand and company.

CHAPTER 3

Making Your Product or Service Sustainable

Two Definitions of Sustainability

To most entrepreneurs, sustainability means building a company that will prosper and survive. Much of corporate America's definition, however, tends to complement—or at least mimic—the EPA's:

> Sustainability is based on a simple principle: Everything that we need for our survival and well-being depends, either directly or indirectly, on our natural environment. Sustainability creates and maintains the conditions under which humans and nature can exist in productive harmony.[1]

Based on the "entrepreneurial" definition of sustainability, entrepreneurial leaders should be asking themselves, "How do I grow and sustain my business in the long term?" Below, I'll share three ways to ensure that your product or service remains sustainable in the entrepreneurial sense, based on my own experiences running several successful long-term enterprises.

Trademarks

A trademark not only distinguishes a product or service from its competitors; it provides legal protection against others using a company's name or logo. Trademarks make it possible for companies to invest energy, effort, resources, and time in building a brand without the fear of others taking advantage of the goodwill created by their efforts.

I learned the value of trademarks very early in my career, when I was able to acquire one national brand franchise for the entire Northeast: Weight Watcher soft drinks. At the time, I was general manager at Bev-Pak.

By 1993 our annual sales had reached 4,800,000 containers. Yet persistent problems seemed to plague our relationship with Weight Watchers, one of them being that they were just entering the food and beverage markets. Another stumbling block was that their image at the time was very strict, not allowing foods that most people enjoy.

In 1978 food giant Heinz Inc., purchased Weight Watchers and ultimately our franchise. Although Heinz didn't have the legal right to do so, they canceled our agreement. We easily could have sued, but I decided to put our energy into a positive effort. With the suggestion of one of my brokers, I decided to introduce "Waist Watchers," in an attractive package with a tape measure shaped around an imaginary waist. Of course I knew before doing this that we had to obtain a trademark.

The product was an instant success. Whereas before we were selling 200,000 cases annually of Weight Watchers, we were now selling this many cases of Waist Watchers on a monthly basis. Our first-year sales exceeded two million cases.

Beware of Trademark Trouble

With our newfound success came a letter in the mail advising me of a lawsuit by Weight Watchers and Heinz for trademark infringement. The lawsuit was for several million with "treble" damages, meaning all damages awarded would be tripled.

I immediately called my New York City trademark lawyer, whose response all but floored me. "Get rid of the product that you have on hand, destroy the labels, and tell them you did this. [Tell them you] won't sell any more if they will drop the suit. This always works." The shock to my system is still impossible to describe: Waist Watchers had become a very important part of our business, and it had a lot of potential. This lawyer was the same man who'd helped me decide on the Waist Watchers name. As I learned that day, not all experts are what they claim to be.

This was the beginning of a long fight that lasted two and half years, with us employing six law firms at one time. It also included seven court appearances. Eventually we won, settling with Weight Watchers out of court for the right to market the Waist Watchers brand throughout the

United States in perpetuity. The brand would end up generating over $12 million in sales annually.

Despite our successes, I wouldn't recommend this to any entrepreneurial leader, because it is very distracting dealing with this many attorneys, large legal fees, meetings, and court appearances while trying to generate new business and run a company. The moral of the lesson? Find real experts on trademark law who can always keep your best interests in mind.

First-Mover Advantage

Establishing first-mover advantage is another way for your company to ensure sustainability. First-mover advantage can be defined as

> a form of competitive advantage that a company earns by being the first to enter a specific market or industry. Being the first allows a company to acquire superior brand recognition and customer loyalty. The company also has more time to perfect its product or service.[2]

Being first and special creates a great deal of free awareness, often due to publicity generated by the news media and word of mouth.

However, first-mover advantage isn't always sustainable, especially when a competitor introduces a product or service that's perceived to be better. Often, a competitor will introduce a "better" product or service quite awhile later and still be recognized as the "first mover." Google, for example, came three years after Yahoo. Intuit, which was thirteenth to enter the personal financial software market with TurboTax, may be the best example of all. It went on to claim a 75 percent market share.[3]

In cases like these, first-mover advantage falls to the company that seems to be the first to have the best product, in the eyes of the consumer. Other companies that excel in establishing "sustainable" first-mover advantage are Procter & Gamble, Gillette, Apple, Microsoft, Intel, and Toyota.

Constant and Continuous Improvement

How do you keep the benefits earned by first-mover advantage? One answer is *constant and continuous improvement* in every area of doing business, including marketing, operations, and finance. The companies that fail to do this lose their first-mover advantage and damage their sustainability.

I was lucky to see an excellent example of constant and continuous improvement, particularly in the area of customer service, by watching the CEO of our can supplier, Crown Cork & Seal. I thought I'd seen it all until I met Mr. Connelly.

For years he answered his own phone calls, so as not to have people be "filtered" by anyone. Any customer could call him directly, and he would pick up the phone and carry on a conversation. When I called him many years later, he was winding down his career and in his late eighties. His company had grown from one whose sales were in the millions to one whose assets were in the billions, so I didn't expect to get him on the line. When I gave my name to his secretary, the call went through instantly. I was floored, in a good way. We were a decent customer, but our purchases were a small fraction of Mr. Connelly's overall business, which included Coke, Pepsi, Budweiser, and other big-name brands.

Later, I once sat in a Harvard economics class with a professor who made the argument that Mr. Connelly built his company on ten-cent cans. I had never challenged a professor, nor would I ever, except for this one time.

"I knew Mr. Connelly personally," I said. "He did not build a company on ten-cent cans; he built it on customer service. He was the definition of customer service."

Mr. Connelly had an amazing record at Crown Cork & Seal, with 84 consecutive quarters of sales and profit increases.

Generating New Business Utilizing Continuous Improvement

Creating products and services is an ideal way of generating new business, but we should never neglect our existing products and services as fertile ground to generate new business. The best and easiest way to accomplish this is through continuous improvement of our existing line of products and services. We only have to look at the examples of Microsoft, with their continuous upgrades of their software products, and Apple, with their new and better iPhones and iPad models. This strategy has worked so well for Apple that they recently became the first company to be worth more than $700 billion.[4]

Continuous Improvement and the Wow Factor

At Adirondack Beverages, our main method of continuous improvement was based on our wow factor. All changes were governed by the rule that "change is not justified unless it can create a 'wow,' or something dramatically better than that of our competitors." Generally speaking, when customers recognize a "wow," that "wow" is a powerful marketing tool for your company.

Creating a "wow" with your internal customers (employees) is also important. Our TQM program created a wow by empowering our people, benchmarking our production efficiencies against world-class standards, elevating our service levels to those of world-class companies, and attempting to reduce consumer complaint letters. Our goal was to have more complimentary consumer letters than complaint letters. We reached this level two years before I sold the company.

We had always prided ourselves on our customer service, but there was one area that needed a "wow," and that was how we handled phone calls. Once, I called the company to speak to one of our leaders without telling the operator who I was. I was put on hold for what seemed like an eternity. I thought to myself, "This is not how Mr. Connelly operated."

Around the same time I just happened to read an article about L. L. Bean's outstanding customer service. When a customer called them, an operator would answer in two rings and give his or her name. Now, that is a world-class "wow."

Following L. L. Bean's lead, we put in a phone system that would beep throughout the office if a person was on hold for more than 20 seconds. If you call Adirondack today, the operator will greet you in two rings or fewer with his or her name.

Most people and companies settle for "good enough," and not excellence. In today's ultracompetitive marketplace, however, "good enough" doesn't cut it, especially with the presence of the Internet and our worldwide communications explosion.

Excellence also won't cut it unless it can be sustained. Protecting intellectual property with patents and trademarks is helpful. Being first can be an advantage; however, it isn't everything, as companies like Google have shown us. Continuous improvement is essential in generating new business from existing products, and it is the one element that will protect and maintain a comparative and competitive advantage. This advantage is essential to sustaining excellence in the highly competitive world we live in.

Closing Thoughts: A Big "Wow" in a Small Way

Mother Theresa once said, "Not all of us can do great things. But we can do small things with great love." Often when I talk about "wows," people think that it has to be an "iPad wow" or something equally spectacular. It doesn't—it can be something as simple as a three-day service guarantee. My friends Luca Cassani and Antonio Pariano, who own and operate Cassariano's Italian Eatery in Venice, Florida, are a great example. Antonio is the chef, and an outstanding one at that. I've been eating delicious Italian food all my life, and he constantly surprises me with dishes I've never tried, and different—and often better—versions of my favorite dishes.

With its beautiful exposed-brick walls, modern circular light fixtures, and hardwood floors, their new restaurant's ambiance reminds me of an upscale New York City restaurant. It's definitely something to tell your friends about. You can also sit outside and enjoy the beautiful Florida weather. The clincher is that Luca greets everyone when they come in, and he also tends to them when they're sitting down. He's very pleasant, knows everyone's name, and never forgets to greet you in a personal manner. Luca makes sure all the staff provide prompt and courteous service.

This all works because it's a surprise! We're not accustomed to being greeted by the owner of a business, let alone one who is pleasant and knows and remembers your name. Also, the setting of Cassariano's is terrific, with an outstanding menu and fantastic food to boot. As we used to say in establishing our TQM program at Adirondack, our goal is to *exceed* customer expectations, and that's what Luca and Antonio excel at.

Just remember—you don't have to be Steve Jobs to create a "wow" and a sustainable business; all you have to do is follow Luca and Antonio's example.

CHAPTER 4

Keeping Your Product or Service Profitable

A long with keeping a business sustainable, an entrepreneur must also be sure it earns a profit. Due to the burden of start-up costs, most new products and services don't make a profit in the short term. Yet in order for a company to prosper, products and services must be profitable over the long term. Good entrepreneurial leaders recognize that sustaining a profit is necessary for a business to grow and survive.

Profit to a business is analogous to what salary and bonuses are to employees. The more talented, skilled, educated, ingenious, and hardworking, the greater the justification for an attractive salary and large bonuses to be earned. This is also true for a business: the more skilled and talented the entrepreneurial leader, the greater the profits.

In the last chapters, we covered some key factors in achieving profitability: securing patents and trademarks, establishing a competitive advantage, and achieving first-mover advantage. Yet keeping a product profitable also means that good business practices must be in place, not only in a company's marketing and process management efforts, but also fiscally.

Three Ways to Avoid Liquidity Problems

One of the most common and difficult problems for new companies is liquidity, or having enough cash to operate. Liquidity problems often surface in companies that are in serious trouble; however, they also can occur in profitable companies—profitable on paper, that is. A company can show a profit when the comptroller produces a financial statement, yet still be out of cash. In this chapter, I'll discuss three ways to keep this from happening: guarding your cash, diligently policing your accounts payable to guard against bad debt, and negotiating beneficial terms from suppliers.

Guarding Your Cash

Guarding your cash means making sure you have enough in reserve to pay your bills, including meeting payroll and covering the mortgage. Failure to make payroll not only may drive away employees but will also destroy your credibility with those who decided to stick with you. And the easiest and surest way for your company to be out on the street is by missing mortgage payments. Also keep in mind that a failure to pay suppliers will result in not being able to obtain materials necessary to produce your products and make delivery.

Guarding your cash is also a good barometer of how well you are doing: if you have a surplus of cash, it's a good indicator that you are fiscally on the right track. Always be sure to keep a close eye on your books. At one point, just before our computerized system came into play at Adirondack, I used to check with our comptroller first thing every morning to see how much money had come into our bank lockbox the previous day. (Our customers would mail their payments to our bank, and the bank would expedite their deposits.) Though my situation was a little unusual, you'll need the same fiscal vigilance as an entrepreneurial leader.

Avoid Unnecessary Debt

Another thing we did during this period was to be careful not to make unnecessary debt and obligations. This principle is just as important when a business is doing well. Often when things are really good and the cash is rolling in, we are tempted to buy things that we don't really need. Before deciding if you can afford something, it is important to ask, "Do we really need this?" If the answer is yes and the item is essential, then the next questions should be, "Does this fit in our budget? What do we have to gain if we buy this item? What do we have to lose if we don't?"

In other words, "Can we afford the payments based on current profits, and can we sustain the payments if we have a drop in our business?" The final question to ask is, "How long will it take us to pay for it?" In other words, how long will you have to deal with this additional payout?

In assessing your liquidity, it's good to remember the saying, "Always keep enough in reserve for a rainy day."

Negotiating Terms with Suppliers

When negotiating terms with suppliers, you should always ask for the longest payment periods possible. When I purchased Adirondack Beverages, I was told we wouldn't be able to obtain credit, because the company was 100 percent leveraged—that is, we'd borrowed 100 percent of the purchase price. In addition to this, our mortgage holder had attached all of our assets, including our inventories of products and materials. This meant that other than our mortgage holder, a bank wouldn't lend us money, because we had no assets to offer as security, since they were already attached. Suppliers also would not be able to claim their products, since they were attached by our lender, and in most cases they would have been used in manufacturing, sold, and out the door.

Surprisingly to most people, we were able to negotiate good payment terms with our suppliers, including discounts. Usually in our industry, creditors would issue a 2 percent discount only if you paid your bill in ten days, versus thirty. However, we were able to negotiate this same discount on payments of up to thirty days. By the third year, we had negotiated 90-day terms with a major supplier.

I believe these terms were made possible because of my reputation, and because our suppliers trusted in our ability to be successful. Over time I've found that, as the saying goes, "It never hurts to ask." I'm always surprised by the results when I do.

Guarding Against Customers' Debt

On the flip side, guarding against *customers'* bad debt often means enacting several measures. The first is conducting a thorough credit screening, as well as reviewing customers' payment histories and credit ratings, if possible. Dun & Bradstreet is, at the moment, pretty much the only business credit report service. Not all credit experts recommend them, however, because their information is primarily based on information submitted by the companies being reviewed. We used them, but I encourage you to exercise caution for this reason.

We also had our own methods to check out our customers' credit, which I'd recommend to any entrepreneurial leader. For large customers, we bought a share of stock in their company, so that we would receive their annual financial reports. For smaller customers, we would require a bank statement, knowing that, by law, the bank can't provide false information. These statements and reports always contained guarded information, but it was possible to read in between the lines.

Another method was to ask for recommendations from suppliers. Although suppliers were also very cautious about revealing sensitive information, we were often able to make a connection with a customer's supplier through a supplier of our own, who would be more likely to provide us with accurate information.

Our most effective method of guarding against bad debt was speeding up payments by our customers. I know what you're probably thinking— *Everyone wants to do this, but how?* Actually the technique isn't that complicated or difficult—it comes down to offering discounted terms for paying promptly, just as we'd previously been offered. If a customer made a payment in ten days, we allowed a 2 percent discount. Instantly, our average payment time went from 34 to 14 days.

Obtaining extended terms from our suppliers was an ideal way to increase our cash reserves; speeding up payments was equally beneficial, increasing our cash flow by a whopping 240 percent. Just as important, discounted terms are an ideal way to prevent bad debt.

It is highly unusual for a large customer to bypass cash discounts. In fact, I don't know of a single customer who ever did, just because it's an easy way to earn cash. Beware: when a company stops taking discounts, it's an alarm that goes out to the trade; most often, bankruptcy follows. Several grocery chains went bankrupt both inside and outside of our territory. Luckily, we didn't experience significant losses, nor did other companies that offered discounted terms. The big losers were the companies with net terms.

As a final precaution against bad debt, we tracked our customers' payment histories. Each month we recorded how long it took for each customer to make payments. If their schedule fell back by even a day and stayed there for two consecutive months, the customer was put on alert. (This meant closer monitoring, including asking friends in the industry if they were having the same experience.) When payment slows down even for a day, it's a sign that a company's cash flow is slowing down, and that's a definite warning sign.

The net result of all of this was that we fortunately never experienced serious losses as a result of bad debt. Our annual losses never reached double figures, an outstanding performance for a company whose annual sales exceeded $60 million.

Banking on an Important Relationship

I have never liked being in debt (does anyone really enjoy it?). This must seem like a really strange comment from a guy who borrowed

100 percent of a multimillion-dollar purchase. Unlike what many people believe, most entrepreneurs don't make a practice of risking everything they have.

Over the 13 years I owned Adirondack Beverages, we invested over $23 million in capital improvements without borrowing a dime. We were able to do this because of the measures I mentioned earlier, and also because we nurtured one critical relationship: that with our bank.

Once we had overcome our initial obstacles and it was clear that we would be successful, we established a relationship with a large blue-chip institution. We had a seven-figure line of credit that we had never used. Also, we had never borrowed from them. We carried large balances, and millions of our dollars flowed through their bank. I knew our bankers were impressed with us, so I figured it would be helpful to negotiate a better and closer relationship with them.

We started by my asking our officer to bring the president of the bank to visit our facility for a tour. When they came I gave them the same tour that I'd give a customer, yet I knew this wasn't a case of selling product: it was a matter of selling us. We needed the president to believe we were credible, because he could save our business in a pinch.

Fortunately the tour and visit went very well. The next step was to borrow $2 million that we absolutely did not need or have any specific use for—an amount in addition to our seven-figure line of credit. This was the easiest part of the relationship; they gave it to us within days. Having $2 million in cash would insure against being denied a loan if business turned sour on a short-term basis.

The most rewarding part of this story is that I became friends with the local president of our bank as well as the president of the regional bank. They were so impressed with our company that when we sold it to one of the oldest and most established investment banking firms in New York City, they fought aggressively to obtain the financing of the purchase. They won and continued as the company's banker.

This story highlights a critical point for entrepreneurial leaders when it comes to dealing with bankers, accountants, lawyers, and all other professionals. These people most often are very influential and have powerful contacts. If they like you and your company, they will pass this on, and it will help tremendously to build your credibility and reputation and those of your company.

Finding and hiring the right professionals can be challenging. It requires the same knowledge, skill set, and process as building a team that will help you generate new business—the topic of our next chapter.

CHAPTER 5

Eight Tips for Effective Team Building

In a new venture—or any venture, for that matter—having an effective team is the most critical factor in determining if the first four steps of my model can be successfully implemented. Good people will recognize a commercially viable problem, help to develop a unique solution, and assure sustainability and profitability. I was lucky, at Adirondack, to have an entire organization dedicated to generating new business and our process.

It started with our regional sales managers in seven states, who were constantly looking for unsolved problems in their markets, problems that were ripe for solutions. This would result in endless ideas that we would work on as team to determine if they were opportunities for Adirondack. More often than not, it involved field trips with team members to specific markets to interview customers. The Adirondack Clear 'n' Natural product line is the direct result of our regional sales managers bringing to my attention a competitor's new and successful product line that could definitely be improved upon.

Our salespeople weren't the only people who brought us ideas. Many ideas came from our production, office, and transportation teams. Our drivers constantly told us about competitors' trucks and conversations with their drivers about their products. "Ange," they'd say, "we need to do this or that. We can do it better than those guys."

The best indicator of how concerned our people were with generating new business and sustaining our company was our open discussion conversations at our companywide quarterly meetings, which our employees were paid to attend (we always had 100 percent participation). The first question in our discussion period was always, "What new products are we coming out with?" After we'd filled our employees in, there'd always be a lively discussion involving every department. My first reaction was, "Wow, we have a company full of entrepreneurial leaders who want to create products." Of course, I also realized it was their future we were talking about.

Having the whole team cooperating willingly is terrific and beneficial to a leader. It's also the best weapon for ensuring sustainability.

* * *

Learning how to assemble a team was one of the most difficult things I've had to do in my life and career. Much of what I learned about leadership and team building came from *not* doing to others what I'd seen done to others and me. In other words, much of what I learned was based on what I *didn't* appreciate.

On the positive side, I enjoyed closely observing successful leaders, whether they were coaches, past presidents, or social leaders. Some of my favorites were George Washington, Abraham Lincoln, FDR, JFK, Dr. Martin Luther King Jr., and Gandhi. I also learned a lot about teamwork from UCLA coach John Wooden and my favorite, Vince Lombardi of the Green Bay Packers. Finally, I learned a great deal by trial and error. It's great to learn how successful people do what they do, but you'll never learn how to do anything yourself until you try to apply everything you've observed.

The following are eight tips on building an effective team, culled from my forty years of practicing leadership and entrepreneurship. Hopefully you'll find them helpful as you begin to assemble your own winning team.

1. Attitude and Character Are More Than 50 Percent; Skills Can Be Taught

I remember being on a dais once with another CEO in a meeting, discussing human relations issues. He mentioned that hiring in his company was based 50 percent on attitude and 50 percent on skill. When it was my turn to speak, I mentioned that our practice was similar but a little different. If a potential employee's attitude and character weren't what we approved of, we never considered his or her skills. Years of experience had taught me that attitudes are very difficult to change. We were looking for positive, can-do people who could work together as a team (not superstar heroes, although we were content if an employee grew into one).

Character is even more important than attitude. I like something I read a long time ago: that "character is what a person does when no one is looking." Good character is a must, because no company has enough time and money to monitor every employee all the time. If a candidate had the right attitude and character, we found that we could teach him or her the skills necessary for the job. If a specific job didn't match up right away, we could find something else for the candidate to do.

Nineteen-year-old Veronica Mattas was a perfect example. After working for us part time while earning her bachelor's degree, she came to us seeking a full-time job upon graduation. Unfortunately, we really didn't have anything for a person with her credentials, but we nonetheless created a job for her at our office. Veronica quickly ascended to become the assistant to the IT manager, then warehouse manager, and after that the transportation manager. Amazingly, even while assuming these additional responsibilities and duties, she managed to earn a master's degree with the help of our educational assistance program. Today—33 years after joining Adirondack Beverages—Veronica is second-in-command at the company. To quote Veronica, "I sensed the feeling that I could make a difference. . . . I want to share a positive attitude with everybody, because attitude is contagious."

2. Know Yourself and What Help You Need

Probably the most difficult person to be honest with is one's self. Most entrepreneurial leaders know their strengths, but they also need to learn their faults, painful as the process can be. Team building has to start with an assessment of both our strengths and weaknesses. Only then can we build a team that fills in the gaps with people who have skills we don't have, and that we need.

At Adirondack, our most challenging position to fill was that of comptroller. Despite being strong in this area, the job wasn't something that I liked to do. However, it was very important to our company.

Our first comptroller was a complete disaster, even though he came highly recommended by an accounting firm. Shortly after we hired him, a near-calamity hit: several of our employees' paychecks bounced. The news spread through our plant like wildfire, and it severely undermined my credibility, considering I'd just boasted that we'd had the resources to make our success happen. To make matters worse, most of the employees with bounced checks had attempted to cash them at grocery stores that were customers of ours, so now the news was also spreading throughout the trade.

Two comptrollers later, I came across Doug Martin, a standout CPA who'd unearthed fraud at his previous company. We were comfortable with Doug from the beginning, but Doug needed about two years to truly feel like an expert about our company. Doug not only achieved this, but also went on to become plant manager. Currently, he's running Adirondack Beverages.

3. Pick People Who Are Better Than You at What You Do

This should be a matter of common sense, but in the words of Mark Twain, "Common sense is not so common." If there are skills you don't have and you pick people no better than you, the team can never improve in these areas, which isn't very good. This can be difficult to carry out in the areas in which you excel. However, I found that no matter how proficient I thought I was, there was always someone better than me. A good example for me was in the area of sales. I felt I was a pretty good salesman and manager, but I had to be honest with myself: when it came to formal presentation skills, I hated using PowerPoint, and although I was good with numbers and details, I didn't enjoy dealing with them.

When it came time to hire a new sales manager, I turned to our internal team. I asked my wife what she thought, since she knew all of our regional managers.

"Frank should be your next sales manager," she said without thinking. "He's a really good person, and you always brag about what a great job he's doing."

I had to admit that Frank Cosenza was an outstanding performer with excellent sales production figures. He was also far better than me in presentation skills and attention to details and numbers. Yet he flew under the radar, because he did his job in a nice, quiet way. I decided to give Frank a chance.

Frank ended up doing an outstanding job for us, and he was able to help us grow the company significantly. Like Veronica and Doug, Frank is still working at Adirondack as a sales manager for private contracting, the largest portion of their business.

4. Be a Team Player—Leave Your Ego at the Door

I have learned that life, leadership, and entrepreneurship are all team sports. As we'll soon explore in the Enduring Leadership Model, willing cooperation from subordinates is what leaders need most to be successful. In other words, an organization should be built around teamwork and team players, not superstars.

I learned early that the easiest thing to give away is credit, and it is appreciated. I remember being asked so many times in post-presentation question-and-answer sessions why everything I mentioned about our programs and successes always started with "we." For example, "Don't *you* ever do anything worthwhile? Why do you always say 'we'?" My answer was, "I'll take credit for hiring our people."

The thing that I think surprised them most was that I was sincere, and our people knew this. Working together as a team, with each person pulling his own weight and then some, is the ideal form of cooperation. And the more people you lead, the more you need your people to cooperate willingly with you and each other.

5. Experience Matters

We were fortunate to have a lot of young leaders who would be with us for a long time. Young people are terrific to have around, because they have a great deal of energy and enthusiasm. They lack one thing, though: experience. I have often heard people say that experience is the best teacher, but I believe this just isn't so. Bad experiences can leave scars that are difficult to overcome.

One of the worst things we can do as leaders is push people too far too fast. Major-league baseball is very aware of this issue. Their minor-league system is there to give young players experience—hopefully positive experience.

I have two very personal examples of the hazards of pushing young people too fast. At 25, I was made a supervisor at Canada Dry, with seven salesmen under me. I knew nothing about how to lead or supervise, and I received very little help or training from my company. Not knowing how to lead or supervise was only the tip of the pile of problems I was to face: every salesman was older than me (the youngest being ten years older), and every one had been with the company longer than I had. To make matters even more interesting, one of them felt shunted and passed over for the promotion.

Since I'd never given a presentation in a work environment, my public speaking skills were problematic. Yet my boss tasked me with making the lead presentation at our holiday kick-off meeting. The holidays were very important to Canada Dry, which was the leading ginger ale and mixer company in the world at the time.

The meeting always brought leaders from both the Canada Dry parent company and from our company. These would be audience members who could keep, promote, or fire me. Also present would be a bunch of salesmen who looked at me as the young guy with less experience who somehow got promoted.

When I got up to speak, absolutely nothing came out, and my knees were shaking. I'll never, for the rest of my life, forget how this felt. Somehow I got through the presentation, but no one was impressed—the understatement of the century.

My well-intentioned boss had overestimated my readiness, and it created a scar that I was to struggle with for some time. Not only did it affect my public speaking, but it also had a negative affect on my sales ability.

I decided it was time to get smart. I joined the Jaycees and took a "Speak Up" class. At the same time, I took private lessons from a young minister who was a terrific speaker. Along with learning some very valuable speaking tools I gained positive experiences in our sessions and at speeches I made at Jaycee events.

As a result of my education, I learned a lot of lessons about preparation, practicing, and knowing your audience. Now, when I look back on my embarrassing moment and negative experiences, I still shudder, but I also realize they provided me with the motivation to get help. When I gave the holiday speech the next year, I was offered an attractive job as a result. I refused the job because I wasn't ready, but I was thankful for learning an important lesson.

6. Mix Experience with Youth

When assembling a team, it's always important to make sure that each department has both young and experienced people. All of one without the other can be fatal. Packing a department with only experienced people who are winding down their careers can make for tired, risk-averse employees. Often these employees are very much set in their ways. All inexperienced people, regardless of their age, become a total learning experience with a little guidance. Mixing the two is an excellent formula: the new people give energy to the more experienced ones, and the experienced ones return the favor by providing wisdom.

When I received my second promotion at Bev-Pak, I had less experience in the new situation than I did during my first promotion. Fortunately, I was to quickly align with Ray Cestar, my production manager. Ray was in his sixties and had been in the beverage industry for over forty years.

I don't know if I would have the patience to put up with someone like me at the time. I asked an endless stream of questions, because that's how I learned. Yet Ray was patient and kind, and he happily assumed the role of teacher when it came to the production of beverages. When it came to the two of us, I had a lot of energy, Ray had knowledge and wisdom, and together we made a really good team.

7. Remember: Partnerships Are Easy to Get Into and Difficult to Get Out Of

Business partnerships are like marriage: easy to get into, and very hard to get out of. I have some simple rules in choosing a partner: First, the "pit"—principles and values—has to be the same. A partner should bring into the organization something that you otherwise could not obtain from an employee. Also, your partner's skill levels should be different from and complementary to yours.

After leading the company for three years by myself I decided to bring in two partners. In doing so I believed that I was following my rules. My former partner Al DiPasqua, for example, was outstanding in the areas of marketing and operations, two of my strengths also. We both had extensive, successful leadership experience, but we had very different personalities. Al was more of an introvert, and I was the opposite. I was the dreamer who had ideas, often probably too many, and Al was the practical person who could help me sift out the ideas and end up with opportunities. I was probably stronger in sales, but Al was a much more experienced buyer.

We decided that I would run the company and Al would take complete charge of buying, while also advising us on marketing and operations. Along with being a mentor, he saved us millions of dollars with his ability, knowledge, experience, and connections. Al was a great example of a person who never would have worked for me or anyone else. He is one of the best things that ever happened to me in both my business and personal life.

On the opposite side of the spectrum was my other partner, whom I'll call "Joe." Joe came into the company at about the same time as Al. We three were close friends and called ourselves the *tre amici*—Italian for "three friends." Joe was brought into the company with a considerable discount on our stock price, a six-figure salary, and excellent benefits.

I made the mistake that many people often make in choosing a partner, in thinking that I could change Joe once we were "married." My partner had been promoted several times at his old company. However, he was never able to keep the new positions and was either moved laterally or demoted. Eventually, he ended up in business for himself. I was absolutely convinced that he had never been in the "right" position, and I was going to "fix" this.

Unbelievably, the day after becoming my partner, Joe stopped taking my calls after hours. This was not only disturbing but also a surprise, as we'd spent the last seven years traveling together—he was what we called our "master broker," which literally meant our sales manager. We'd talk in person or on the phone at least once every day, including weekends.

Two weeks after becoming partner, Joe initiated divorce proceedings against his wife of several years. Our own relationship took a dramatic turn for the worse and was never the same. It was difficult to have him complete tasks and take charge of his area of responsibility, and it took three years and a lot of money—three to four times what he paid for his stock—to remove him as a partner.

My biggest mistake in this situation was overlooking the fact that our "pits" were different. I remember one day walking in on him during a phone conversation with a customer. He put the customer on hold, and I asked him what was going on. "I am making up the truth as we go along and have to figure out what it is." I'm no saint, but my word is my bond. I was, needless to say, appalled by his behavior.

I'm reluctant to include this story, and I'm sure my former partner has his side of the story as well. It's included because it's a lesson, and a very dramatic one at that. I hope you'll learn by reading this. I also included it because even though I was very good at understanding people, I was still fooled.

8. Control Matters

As you move forward with choosing your partners, keep in mind one critical factor: control. Maintaining control of the ownership in your company should be a major factor. I became an entrepreneur because I wanted my freedom more than anything. As an entrepreneur, the last thing you need is for partners to have control over you and your company. Approaching your affairs this way doesn't mean you don't want your partners' participation and cooperation, just that you won't relinquish your authority.

Two considerations are very important: the first is control of the operations of a company, and the second is the right to sell without consent from minority partners. At one time 51 percent provided operating control, and 67 percent allowed the sale of a company without the permission of minority stockholders. While these numbers may still apply to some business situations, be sure to check with your state. My advice would be to focus on your company's bylaws and shareholder agreement.

Bylaws

Bylaws are an important tool for all organizations. They are a legal document that outlines the rules that govern an organization, while providing guidelines for running the company.

The Shareholder Agreement

The shareholder agreement is a more general agreement outlining how a company should be operated, in addition to the rights and obligations of shareholders. It also regulates the shareholder arrangements (how shareholders shall interact), the management structure, the breakdown of ownership of shares, and the privileges and protection they provide.

One of my guest speakers, whom I'll call Bill, drove home the value of shareholder agreements to my class and me. Bill created a high-tech software company that developed a purchasing program that literally saved millions of dollars for companies. He was successful in raising $43 million from a venture capitalist firm for his start-up while maintaining his position as president and a minority interest in the company (20 percent).

In a very short period of time—12 to 18 months—the company acquired several major accounts, including Walmart. However, it just as quickly ran into financial problems. Bill's major selling point, "guaranteed savings," required "custom individualized programming" rather than a "one-size-fits-all" approach. This approach turned out to be very costly. The company's commitment of guaranteed financial savings required countless hours of costly programming.

A major stumbling block was determining the right price to offer and commit to it in landing the major accounts. If priced too high, the customer most likely would not sign up; if priced too low, Bill's company would lose money. It didn't help that Bill's company wasn't familiar with their customers' internal operations during the bidding process, nor could they be, since each account had its own purchasing system, special circumstances, and agreements.

The losses were substantial: the bigger the account, the more hours of programming required. By the time they had become experts at this process, they had run out of working capital. It was little consolation that all start-ups are a learning process. They would need to raise money and do it soon.

Unfortunately the venture funding market temporarily dried up due to the dot-com bubble that peaked at the end of the 1990s and crashed by 2002. Unable to raise the much-needed capital, the venture fund that had purchased his company decided to sell Bill's company.

Under normal circumstances, Bill, no longer a majority stockholder (51 percent) would have no voice in deciding whether the company should be sold, or in deciding the sale price. However, Bill had written into the bylaws and shareholder agreement that his consent was necessary for all major decisions. By doing this, he had literally maintained control over the key issues his company would be dealing with. A sale certainly qualified.

Although the company was sold at a substantial loss (the sale price was $22 million), Bill was able to negotiate a fair settlement and personal agreement. He was retained as president of the company and received a seven-figure buyout for his minority stock.

The lesson? Remember to maintain control of your company, including the "right to sell," through your bylaws and shareholder agreement.

* * *

Unfortunately, there's no way that I know of to keep score of how well you're doing when you're building a team and creating your company's most important documents. I know this—the outstanding individuals mentioned above helped us make our company into one of the largest independent bottlers in the country. Incredibly, many are still with the company.

In closing this chapter, I feel very much like I'm shutting the door on a part of my life that was very dear to me. Though leaving the beverage industry to move to a different career was very rewarding, leaving our people was much more difficult. For a long time (much longer than I'd like to admit), a sense of loss would come over me when I least expected it. My only consolation is that we built a terrific team, and that many individuals became my friends in the process.

Conclusion

To sum up the five steps in our Opportunity Model, entrepreneurial leaders must do the following:

- **Find a Commercially Viable Problem.** This is the first and most critical step in recognizing an opportunity. Remember, pursuing ideas that are not opportunities is a sure path to failure.

- **Develop a Unique Solution to That Problem.** Your solution must be unique (comparatively better that what's currently on the market) and special. A "wow" is what we're looking for.
- **Ensure That the Solution Is Sustainable.** Sustainability is another word for surviving. Trademarks, patents, and continuous improvement will assure that you'll thrive and survive.
- **Make Sure That the Solution Becomes Profitable, Over the Long Term.** Profit is more than gratifying: it is one of the keys to surviving. Profit is to a company what a salary is to an employee.
- **Build an Effective Team.** An effective team is essential when obtaining financing, and when starting and growing a business. A happy life and a successful business are both team exercises.

In the next chapter, we'll explore how to keep your team happy and productive by implementing what I call professional leadership and personal leadership, the two major components of my Enduring Leadership Model.

Part II

THE ENDURING LEADERSHIP MODEL

CHAPTER 6

Built to Last: The Enduring Leadership Model

In 1993, I sold Adirondack Beverages and decided to further pursue my education and earn a PhD from the University of Albany. As part of my doctoral studies, I reviewed existing research on leadership. What a difference it was to see leadership through an academic lens, rather than as a young boy climbing up from the bottom of a beverage company!

So many of the books I read were biographies and autobiographies. Eager to hear what the "experts" had to say about leadership, I devoured a hundred years' worth of writing on the subject. What I discovered was stunning: in all the literature I read, not a single model or theory captured all the basics of leadership in one place. Very few books even mentioned leadership basics at all! If they did, the mentions were scattered and not part of a cohesive model or theory. The most comprehensive book I could find on leadership was written 35 years ago, by political scientist James Macgregor Burns. A chapter in his book *Leadership*, called "In Search of a General Theory," has been the cornerstone in leadership researchers' quests ever since.

No wonder no one could cite any articles or books for me!

How could this be? How could any profession or skill be taught without starting off with the basics? I simply couldn't understand this. A hint to my questions' answers came in one of my readings. According to leadership expert Warren Bennis, there are over 850 definitions of leadership—each with its own explanation of what makes an effective leader.[1] He goes on to say, "Literally thousands of empirical investigations of leaders have been conducted in the last seventy-five years alone, but no clear unequivocal understanding exists as to what distinguishes leaders from nonleaders, and perhaps more important, what distinguishes *effective leaders* from *ineffective* leaders and *effective* organizations from *ineffective* organizations."

Considering that experts can't even agree on what leadership *is*, let alone *how* it should be practiced, it's no wonder that we have such a difficult time teaching leadership. Our gap in understanding culminates with the ineffective leaders we see every day in the business and political worlds. My goal here is simple: I want to share my unique leadership model with you, so that you can build an effective team and a successful organization. The Enduring Leadership Model is a general theory that outlines the fundamentals of entrepreneurial leadership. The model fills a gap that exists in the extant leadership literature.

This model was developed by many years of practicing successful leadership myself, by studying effective leaders up close and personal,

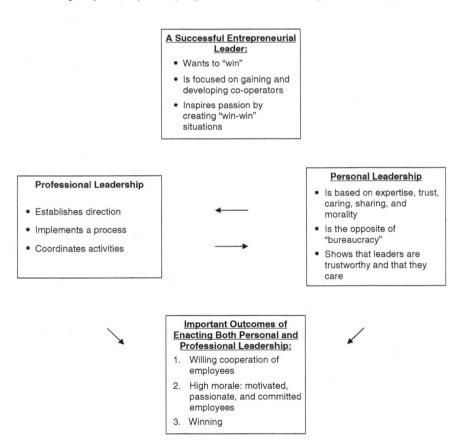

Figure 6.1   The Enduring Leadership Model for Entrepreneurs

and by reading as much business and academic literature as I could. My sincere wish is that this model will help lay the groundwork for you, as a future entrepreneur and business leader.

The Enduring Leadership Model is quite simple to summarize, yet it is exceptionally difficult to put into practice. The model emphasizes "personal leadership"—the character and characteristics of leaders—over more "formal" aspects of leadership, which I refer to as "professional leadership." Professional leadership tends to fixate on bureaucracy and other more "process-oriented" aspects of leading an organization.

What Good Leaders Want: The Art of Willing Cooperation

The Many Ways to Win

Let's begin at the top of our "Enduring Leadership" table. What do good leaders want? Obviously, a successful leader wants to "win." "Winning" is easy to measure in the worlds of sports, games, and academia. However, "winning" in a business context can take many forms. It could mean improved efficiency, a greater market share, or—most common today—maximizing profits and shareholder value.

In the context of quality entrepreneurial leadership, "winning" is a long-term prospect. It means creating exciting new products or services that will endure and that will become world-class. It also means, in many cases, becoming the market leader and the best company in the world in the entrepreneur's chosen field.

No matter how "winning" is measured, entrepreneurial leaders want a part of it! But can leaders "win" by themselves? Of course not! A good leader needs good people, and for those people to *cooperate,* and *contribute their efforts*. The more people a leader leads, the more he or she will depend on those people.

Three Ways to Gain Cooperation

Over the past 20 years, I've spent countless hours examining the ways in which leaders earn cooperation. I've never found more than three. We'll start with the most frequently used and end with the most effective and enduring.

Coercion

I wish it weren't true, but the method most often used is coercion. Simply put, coercion is forcing people to do something they'd otherwise not do. Its main goal is compliance, and its main method is discipline (or the threat of discipline). Historically, we've seen coercion most visibly in "unstable" governments, such as Nazi Germany, Stalin's Soviet Union, and many of our present-day Middle Eastern countries.

In a business context, coercion most often takes the form of bosses telling their employees, "If you want to keep your job, you will do it our way." (You could also substitute "promotion" for job.) Supervisors enforce coercion by sharing examples of people who've lost their jobs as a result of not doing things "their way." These same supervisors will also make threats about those who've spoken the truth to their bosses and told them something they didn't want to hear.

At C&C Cola, where I worked for a time, coercion took another form. If a project you led failed, it went on your record and your chances of being promoted were zero. In his book *In Search of Excellence,* the highly regarded business expert Tom Peters explains the C&C phenomenon: "The dominant culture in most big companies demands punishment for a mistake, no matter how useful, small, or invisible."[2]

If a single mistake will ruin your career, then it's no wonder why managers in large companies are risk-averse. One of the most disturbing characteristics of these cultures is that the best way to advance is to not do anything risky or significant. Taking it a step further, many employees are reluctant to even *associate with* anything perceived as challenging or risky.

* * *

While coercion is the most common method of instilling cooperation in business environments, we can understand why it's also the least effective. I also saw this firsthand at my own company, Adirondack Beverages, when we tried to implement a program against theft.

At Adirondack, we had a popular policy called the "Free Soft Drink for Personal Use" program, where each employee was entitled to two cases a week of free soft drinks. An unfortunate by-product of the program was pilferage, which we tried to correct through coercion. Though "excess" soft drink pilferage was a relatively minor problem for us, monetarily speaking, it was still annoying, disappointing, and time-consuming. We vowed to put an end to it immediately. In addition to installing cameras throughout our facilities, we started randomly surveying our inventory. I also held frequent meetings with our "head grape"—the person in our company who wasn't a formal leader but who had the inside scoop on everything and everyone.

Nothing worked. Not the cameras, not the surveys, and certainly not the meetings with our head grape, who was reluctant to divulge any information. We decided to try another tack: letting our people solve the problem for us. Our plant manager argued that losses from pilferage were the result of actions by our employees. Therefore, the penalties should come out of our "employee incentive program." I agreed. This program was set up to give everyone a "piece of the pie" if things went well: if an employee suggestion or employee-initiated program saved us money, then we'd give half of those savings back. Now, unfortunately, we'd have to do the reverse.

We notified our people of this change at our weekly meetings with their leaders, as well as through a notice in their paychecks—a standard procedure of ours. At the same time, we earnestly asked for our employees' help, telling them the truth—that we didn't want to fire anyone, just to stop the pilferage. Most importantly, we emphasized that we would depend on *them* to solve the problem.

Immediately after we made this announcement, the pilferage stopped. To quote President Eisenhower, "You do not lead by hitting people over the head—that's assault, not leadership."

Material Exchange

Our experience with our "Free Soft Drink for Personal Use" policy demonstrated both the ineffectiveness of coercion and the efficacy of our next method for gaining cooperation: material exchange.

"Material exchange" means giving a person something in exchange for his or her efforts. This is a popular method in business and can include monetary compensation, promotions, stock options, and various other perks.

In order to be effective, material exchange requires a sensitivity to employees' emotions and much fine-tuning on the part of management. We learned this lesson the hard way when we first began compensating our 18-wheeler drivers.

Originally, our drivers had been paid on an hourly-based system, which provided an incentive for drivers to earn as many hours as possible. Since the Department of Transportation controlled the amount of hours truck drivers could work, our drivers quickly began to have availability problems. It wasn't uncommon for our drivers to "run out of hours" (a phenomenon also experienced by airline pilots). We also began to experience problems with getting trucks back in time for next-day deliveries.

Clearly, we needed to do something, or our whole distribution system would collapse, leaving us with a lot of unhappy employees on our hands. Our solution was to create a per-trip pay scale. We calculated the amount of time reasonably and legally required for each delivery in our seven-state market territory. We then determined a reasonable payment for each trip. At first, the drivers were suspicious of the change, but they agreed to go along with it. We assured them that their pay would increase, and that we'd make adjustments if it didn't.

The result was that all of our trucks returned from their deliveries in a reasonable and workable time frame. The drivers' pay increased while their hours decreased, benefiting both them and our company. It was a win-win situation for all.

Persuasion and Willing Cooperation

Finally, the third and most enduring method of ensuring cooperation, after coercion and material exchange, is persuasion. The state of being effectively persuaded is something I call "willing cooperation." The best way I can describe what I call "willing cooperation" is for people to *want to* contribute their efforts toward achieving the common purpose of the organization. Employees who willingly cooperate have, in general, high morale. As an entrepreneurial leader, you want to inspire willing cooperation whenever possible.

At Adirondack, we enacted "willing cooperation" when we changed our hourly production schedule. Originally, like most production facilities, our employees worked eight-hour shifts over five-day spans. Then we began experimenting with a four-day workweek consisting of ten-hour shifts. Our managers loved the change! Since Friday became employees' "overtime" day, any fears they had about work interfering with weekend plans quickly dissipated, resulting in a much happier atmosphere overall.

On top of the new three-day weekend, the four-hour gap between shifts meant more time for performing routine maintenance. This prevented both machine breakdowns and lost production time, resulting in increased productivity and savings to us.

But there was a snag. Legally, according to our union contract, we were required to pay time-and-a-half for the extra two hours of our ten-hour days. This was something we simply couldn't afford. Paying time-and-a-half would nullify any savings we'd enjoyed from the increased productivity. Unless the employees consented to being paid the regular rate for all ten hours with time-and-half kicking in over forty hours, then we'd have to go back to the eight-hour shifts.

So we put it to a vote. The employees overwhelmingly voted for the ten-hour day, even with regular pay. The ten-hour day is still being utilized today.

How to Develop Co-Operators

At this juncture, it's important to remember two points about entrepreneurial leadership: First, leaders want to win. Second, leaders need the willing cooperation of employees—whom we'll call "co-operators"—to win. Therefore, the most important question now is, "How can leaders develop these co-operators?"

We develop co-operators by being passionate and enthusiastic about our messages. Co-operators are very good at detecting real passion (and the lack thereof). Like the co-operators of spiritual leaders such as Gandhi and King, today's entrepreneurial co-operators are keenly attuned to whether their leaders show passion and enthusiasm.

I'd understand the value of this lesson later in my career, when I became frustrated by not being allowed to be entrepreneurial. Being entrepreneurial, for me, equates with being passionate and enthusiastic. I was general manager at Bev-Pak (the previous name of Adirondack), and the market was changing. Customers were demanding the larger two-liter bottle size. Unfortunately, our owner had traded our rights away to make this new, hugely popular design.

Unfortunately, there wasn't a whole lot I could do. Needless to say, it was difficult to be enthusiastic about selling a product that I knew was dying. Luckily, the problem solved itself when Bev-Pak was sold and I was also "traded" in the deal.

The Power of Win-Win

In today's world, simply being passionate about the company's purpose—its mission and vision—isn't enough. The mission and vision themselves must align to form a win-win situation for both owners and employees, a concept made popular by MIT management professor Douglas McGregor. In his book, *The Human Side of Enterprise*, McGregor calls a win-win situation the "Principle of Integration," or employee engagement.[3] Employee engagement occurs when workers can achieve their own goals *best* when their efforts contribute to the success of the company. In effect, the employees win when the company wins.

Entrepreneurial leaders in companies of all sizes, particularly mid-size and large ones, must ask themselves, "Will co-operators be passionate about my company if it's posting record profits at the expense of their pay? Will they support pay levels that are comparable to what employees earned in the eighties? Would *I* support such policies?" People will not become co-operators if they don't "buy into," accept, and take hold of their leaders' messages, especially those concerning compensation.

Kurt Lewin, considered by many to be the "father of social psychology," argues that people have to be motivated to change. He illustrates motivation by using the example of how frozen ice melts and refreezes.[4] According to Lewin, "melting" represents getting people to reexamine their often strong assumptions about how things are done. Once people have "melted," they need a positive direction that will help them mold new beliefs about new programs. Getting people's "ice" to "refreeze" means that the new programs have to be supported and "lived" by management on down.

I have to warn you that making change this way takes more time up front. It requires involving a lot of people, and the more input you give them, the more time it takes, especially when you first start operating this way. In many cases, people have waited a long time to have a voice, and they usually need to get a lot of issues out of their system. However, from that point on, this way of operating pays dividends in that it requires far fewer adjustments. By using this system, you'll "fix" problems before they even start.

In our case, programs once took three months to plan and six to nine months to refine. By involving our people, programs took us six months to plan and very seldom more than three months to refine.

We also found something much more valuable. First, there was much less aggravation caused to all of us and especially our team members. You see, in the past when we made adjustments, our people were being asked to make mostly little but constant changes, most of which were caused by oversight. Now with the input from the people, we fixed issues that would never become a problem.

The biggest benefits were that the program's chances of success increased dramatically and everyone was much happier. Having worked my way up through the system was very helpful—I never liked to be told to follow without questioning or being able to provide input.

People should never be asked or required to follow blindly—our next topic of discussion.

* * *

In academic literature, a popular term for co-operators is "followers." Personally, I dislike the term. If a leader is heading straight for a cliff, then the last thing he or she needs is for people to follow. Leaders need co-operators who will grab them by the shirt and alert them when there's a cliff ahead. In order to be effective, leaders must be dependent on co-operators at all levels of the organization—co-operators who will provide constructive feedback. Engaged co-operators do more than follow—they willingly contribute their efforts and thoughts.

Another in-vogue phrase is "leading from behind." This phrase is often used to criticize leaders, when in fact leaders are working behind the scenes to obtain buy-in from critical stakeholders. Being out front with no one to follow you or cooperate with you isn't leading: it's going it alone.

In reviewing the methods of gaining co-operators, it's important to remember that we're all born with free will. Respecting it is at the heart of getting people to willingly cooperate. To quote renowned leadership author Chester Barnard,

> The idea of free will is inculcated in doctrines of personal responsibility, of moral responsibility, and of legal responsibility. This seems necessary to preserve a sense of personal integrity.[4]

He went on to say, "We are all in this together, and if you will cooperate, everyone else will respond in kind."

Preventing Catastrophe through Willing Cooperation

When people cooperate willingly, amazing things can happen. We saw this with our own eyes when we tried to fix a problem that had been plaguing the entire beverage industry.

For far too long, the ink applied to the bottom of our cans was getting smeared. The ink spelled out a code that notified us of the time and day the can had been produced, as well as the plant the can had come from. This smearing of the ink was especially problematic, because these codes were essential for proper rotation and quality evaluations. Interestingly, we seemed to find the problem everywhere, including on major beer brewers' products, as well as on the bottom of major soft drinks. No one seemed capable of solving the problem. Since the industry was constricting and becoming a "small industry," number-wise, a tiny group of engineers from the equipment companies was responsible for designing all of our production lines.

After we started our program, one of our production employees submitted a suggestion with a detailed solution to the ink problem. He proposed moving the coding machine to provide more space before reaching the packaging machine, so as to allow more drying time. When I heard about this, I asked him how long he'd had this idea. He said several years.

"Why didn't you tell anyone?" I asked.

"Because I didn't think anyone cared. The managers never asked the production workers about it, nor did they ever listen to us."

"So, why now?" I asked.

"Well, this time I think you guys are serious, or at least it seems that way. So, I thought I'd give it a try."

His solution worked. For the most part, the other companies' cans remained unreadable.

* * *

In the next chapter, I'll show you how what I call "professional leadership" can help you recruit faithful and loyal co-operators, just like the ones Barnard envisioned, and just like our very own at Adirondack Beverages. But first, we'll take a look at every entrepreneur's greatest enemy: bureaucracy.

CHAPTER 7

Professional Leadership: Purpose, Process, Coordination, and Planning

Battling Bureaucracy: Missing the Million-Dollar Call

One memorable morning in the late 1970s, a high-level meeting I was attending was interrupted by a most intriguing call. At the time, I was working for C&C Cola as the plant manager for what had previously been Bev-Pak.

"Sir," said the president's secretary as she stepped in, "Marty [our sales manager] has a call. ShopRite is on the phone. They want to buy one hundred truckloads of our product for a sale this weekend and need to talk to you."

All of us "soft drink guys" gasped. One hundred truckloads meant an order somewhere in the range of $1 million! Surely the president would jump right in on this very important call.

"I'm sorry," said the president, who'd been brought into C&C from the insurance industry. "Marty can't take the call now. Tell them he's in a meeting."

I sighed to myself. Our president was so obsessed with "controlling his meetings" that not even this call could interrupt one!

* * *

As this example demonstrates, the biggest impediment to carrying out effective "professional leadership"—the more formal, process-oriented aspects of running a company—is bureaucracy. Famed social theorist

Max Weber calls bureaucracy the "iron cage" of rule-based, rational control:

> It is primarily the capitalist market economy which demands that the official business of administration be discharged precisely, un-ambiguously, continuously, and with as much speed as possible. . . . Normally, the very large, modern capitalist enterprises are themselves unequalled models of strict bureaucratic organization.[1]

Weber cautions that bureaucracy will forever imprison human choices and identity, telling us, "Perhaps it will so determine [the lives of all individuals] until the last ton of fossilized coal is burnt."

In my experience, the best and easiest way to eliminate bureaucracy is to become an entrepreneur. The entrepreneur's freedom to innovate without bureaucratic restrictions is a major reason why entrepreneurial leadership is where, for the most part, innovation takes place.

In closing, I must note that not all aspects of bureaucracy are bad. After all, what kind of business environment would we have without rules and structure, laws and order? How would people know what was expected of them without job descriptions? And how would anything get done without someone having the authority to make final decisions? Without these sorts of guidelines, employees and leaders would get lost in confusion.

The key to good bureaucracy is making decisions that are rational and calculated, rather than those based on emotions or personal beliefs. They should also be objective and based on facts. Appreciating the positive elements of bureaucracy is essential to understanding professional leadership, the first major component of my Enduring Leadership Model.

Professional Leadership

Creating a Common Purpose

Professional leadership encompasses the "formal" part of leadership—setting the vision and mission for an organization, and creating a process for achieving the organization's goals. Creating such a process typically means that a leader will align procedures, people, and infrastructure. It will also mean that a leader will establish a "common purpose."

In my experience, establishing a "common purpose"— a reason to exist, and a collective vision of what the company strives to be—is the most important and most difficult task set out for the entrepreneurial leader.

Proactive Communication: Mission, Vision, and Method of Operations Statements

Establishing a common purpose starts with *proactive communication.* Proactive communication is the art of telling team members what's expected of them in advance, rather than reacting to their actions in a given situation. The best way to accomplish proactive communication is through creating the following:

1. A **mission statement** giving your reasons for existing
2. A **vision statement** outlining where you'll be in five years
3. A **method of operations statement** explaining how the company will deal with both its external and internal customers

After attending the OPM program at Harvard, it became apparent to me that we needed to change despite the fact that we were very successful. We had been growing at the incredible rate of 30 to 55 percent a year for several years; however, it was becoming much more difficult for us to grow. The program helped me to realize that we were not "entitled" to growth; we need to develop reasons to grow.

It also became clear that we had lost our focus and were caught up in trying every method to obtain growth, with little consideration for the long-term impact our actions would have on the company. Our solution was to implement our TQM (total quality management) program at Adirondack. What we were missing was a formal structure and effective communication of our principles.

I knew that it was time to formalize our method of operating by creating a program and to begin practicing proactive communication. I asked our leaders to develop mission, vision, and method of operations statements that could be presented on one sheet of paper.

The leaders understood that they were to give our employees the opportunity to have input on these issues as well. Our people knew our reasons to exist: to provide our customers with the best value in the soft drink section, and to be the best independent soft drink company in the world. All they had to do was put our reasons for existing into writing. That way, we could have a clear, concise written message that all of us could live by.

The Pursuit of Excellence

It was a challenge to convince our people that our TQM program, which we called "The Pursuit of Excellence," wasn't just another "flavor of the month." So often, companies start new programs based on some whim of management, only to drop the initiative when the next new program comes along.

In order to get our people's attention, I knew we needed to take extreme action. First, we shut down the plant in the middle of the week. (In our 25 years of business, we'd never lost a day of work, other than on holidays.) Next, we took every employee to the best banquet center in the area, where we held a meeting that introduced our new program. Its full name, "The Pursuit of Excellence: A Lifelong Journey" emphasized a key point in our quest to become the best independent soft drink company. Perfection wasn't possible, but excellence was. Excellence was ultimately what we were after. A "Lifelong Journey" was our message to our people and customers that this was not a quick fix but a change in the way we operated and lived from this day on.

At the beginning, our leaders tried to convince me that we'd need six months to finish our "statements." Though I always gave lots of consideration to the wishes of our leaders, I knew that if we put it off that long, it'd never happen. We would shortly be in the midst of our busiest season, and in the hustle and bustle of doing business, the statements would go by the wayside. I gave our leaders three months to complete the project. We wanted it done before the start of our rush period.

Other than the compressed timeline, our leaders had no objections to our new program. Their one complaint was not being allowed more sheets of paper to put down all of our very critical principles. We compromised, and our "statement sheet" became a pamphlet folded into two. We called it "The Adirondack Way: How Can We Make It Better?" (Appendix B). On the left, we wrote down our mission statement and what we believed in, and on the right, we wrote down our rules of operations.

We asked each employee to keep that pamphlet with him or her at work. That way, if an employee saw me, another leader, or a fellow employee doing something that we didn't commit to, he or she could wave the paper in front of us and point out what we did wrong.

Acting Proactively: The "Living Business Plan"

In the end, the pamphlet didn't suffice on its own. Since "actions speak louder than words," we had to institute programs that would force us to *act* proactively—not just communicate proactively. Our first was what we called a "living business plan," based on a concept I'd learned in a strategic management class at Harvard. As my professor, Phil Thurston, had said, "The problem with business plans is that they most often end up in a drawer gathering dust. For a business plan to be effective, it must be a living document."

Despite my sad experiences with business planning while at C&C Cola, I decided to give Thurston's "living business plan" concept a try. I asked each leader to develop an "operational plan" for the upcoming year, beginning with predictions for sales figures. Then I asked all the department leaders to note in their plans how they'd develop programs to meet their sales projections, including how they'd allocate production crews. Each plan had to include justifications for the leader's estimated figures.

Our "living document" would be used to review each month's operational systems and would be adjusted based on sales performance. For example, we'd previously agreed that 14 people—including forklift drivers, quality control personnel, and maintenance personnel—constituted a production line. Per our "living document," we agreed that the new number of production line personnel should correspond with sales figures. However, we also agreed that we couldn't change this number without the approval of all leaders involved.

After tackling our projected sales figures, we zeroed in on our production-scheduling program. Scheduling the production of more than 400 items was a nightmare, especially because some items required a four- to five-week lead time for acquiring supplies—that, and since we guaranteed 100 percent delivery of our products if we were given three days' notice or more. High-speed equipment such as our can line, which produced 1,200 cans a minute (a case of cans each second!), also didn't help.

Again, we relied on the past, comparing sales figures from the last 13 weeks and the previous year. We created a way to predict sales figures for the upcoming week and month. Throughout this whole process, human input was a necessity. Our salespeople agreed to stay on top of providing production with upcoming promotion dates and projections.

We also agreed, as part of our overall TQM program, to review our performance with each of our customers every quarter. We'd show them how many times we met our standards—i.e., our promise to them—and how many times we didn't. If we didn't, we promised to do our best to prevent not meeting those standards again. Amazingly, our "satisfaction rate" ended up being very close to 100 percent, including deliveries made within one to two days' notice. Clearly, our customers had come to rely on us in a pinch.

"We Are the Best!"

When we told a major customer that we wanted to be "world-class" and that we wanted to benchmark ourselves against market leaders, we asked who the best companies were. Their answer? "*You* are the best!" This was most gratifying, especially considering that we were benchmarking against huge companies like Procter & Gamble.

The net results and rewards of our "proactive" TQM programs were astonishing to us. Before this process, we solved 70 percent of our problems by reacting and 30 percent by proactively planning. Afterward, we reversed these numbers completely: we ended up solving 70 percent of our problems proactively, before they even started. This saved us a great deal of time and stress—all of which made up for my insisting that we start our program in the middle of our busiest season.

Seeing Bev-Pak's "Big Picture"

Those establishing a common purpose must be able to see the big picture. For me, this immediately kicked in when I became a general manager at Bev-Pak. Bev-Pak was in big financial trouble and in desperate need of sales. We were losing thousands of dollars monthly on a steady basis, and although the owner could afford the losses, he had lost his patience and desire to continue in this direction. My job was to develop a program that would provide the sales and revenue for us to survive, while also getting everyone in the company to pull together.

My immediate supervisor told me that I had until the end of our fiscal year (September 30, a total of seven months) to turn this around, or the plant would be shut down. Needless to say, the stakes were high.

During my first meeting with our department heads, I told them that I didn't know much about their jobs, but that I'd learn as many facts about what they did in a hurry. As I reminded them, the most important thing was for us to work together to solve our problems. I'd provide the marketing programs, and together we'd develop an overall strategy.

What struck me was how each department head was focused on his or her area, and that area only. When I tried to get each department head to make an effort in following the program, he or she would say, "So and so in the other department isn't doing his share." I was amazed at how they could be so focused on others at this time of crisis, rather then on themselves and their people. We weren't a large company, and things were pretty much wide open. In other words, everyone could see what the others were doing.

In their defense, the department heads hadn't had a lot of good experiences in the past. Aside from the production manager, not one of them had any history with me. I knew that I'd have to earn their trust.

The immediate challenge was getting them to understand that we had to work together to save the company. If we didn't, their departments—and, for that matter, their jobs—would cease to exist.

I tried to stay calm. "Do your job, and focus on your people and department," I told my leaders. "Let me do the rest. I assure you everyone will be treated the same and fairly. The good news is that you can and will be a witness to all of this, so you can hold me to my word."

The fact that I didn't have any knowledge in several areas of the company made my challenge that much more difficult. I only knew limited things about manufacturing, transportation, and office management—not to mention the fact that I'd never been a general manager.

Despite all of this, I was confident that we could turn the company around. I was comfortable with my ability to create sales and, even more importantly, to get along with and motivate people. I believed that I could get everyone to work together as a team.

"Everyone has a voice in this," I told the department heads, who looked like they'd just gotten off a 20-hour flight. (We were all being run pretty ragged.) "Make your suggestions; argue your points. But once we settle on what we believe is the right plan, then the talking is over, and we work together to make it a success. No one can change our plan, including me, without coming together and agreeing on the change."

The first program we instituted wasn't a sales program—it was a program to clean the plant. Most people may not realize it, but even when funds are flowing in, it's difficult to keep a manufacturing plant clean. Like with many struggling companies, many of the indirect tasks that weren't involved in the direct sale, manufacture, and delivery of our products had been cut back. This included cleaning. (I should note that this was management's decision, not the employees'. Management is always responsible for these sorts of decisions, because they and only they have the authority to decide what functions to spend their money on.)

I decided that it was important to prove to our leaders, and to everyone in the company, that we could work together successfully and keep the plant spotless. We were getting ready to enter our busiest period of the year, and personally I also wanted to prove that I could make things happen. Two general managers before me had failed, and I was determined not to repeat their mistakes. I believed that we could create sales, but I *knew* we could clean the plant and keep it that way.

As I learned in a leadership seminar for supervisors, the first step in setting a new task is to "make the task important." We started by having all of our leaders explain *why* cleaning the plant was important. (*For God's sake*, I thought to myself, *this is a food plant, after all—I hope they come up with some reasons!*) Then we hammered out *how* we were going to do it. The "how" was actually easy; finding the time to clean when the plant wasn't operating was the tough part.

We also recognized that keeping the plant clean would be a challenge. One of the best tools we used to accomplish this was our "Picking It Up" policy.

"If you see it, pick it up," went the policy, which we reinforced with signs around the building and verbal reminders by all of our leaders. "If it needs more than picking up, tell a leader."

We encouraged everyone, especially the leaders, to look for objects on the floor, and also for areas that needed cleaning. I would purposely walk through the plant and pick up anything that was on the ground, making sure that a leader also knew about these areas. It was important for our people to see that cleanliness started with me, and that I wasn't above getting my hands dirty.

We cleaned the plant and kept it that way, which went a long way in restoring some pride and confidence in our company. People finally understood that if we were going to survive, we had to work together. Unbeknownst to me at the time, I'd just taken our first steps in establishing our company's *common purpose*.

* * *

In my experience, it's far from obvious to the entrepreneur that establishing a common purpose should be a priority. Starting a business, fighting for survival, and heading up a turnaround are all very draining—especially with the failure rates of companies like ours. (In the 1970s, there were 6,000 independent beverage plants in the country; by the time of our TQM program in 1989, it was down to 2,613—a drop of 57 percent.) In the middle of situations like ours, it's very difficult to see the big picture. I remember tense conversations during this time with my mentor, Carl Touhey, the owner of Bev-Pak. He desperately tried to get me to focus on the real problems at hand.

"Ange," he said, "you're so busy trying to fight all the battles of running this company that it's difficult for you to focus on the big picture. I'm not there in the middle of everything, so it's easy for me to see things."

Later, I came to see what I was facing as being similar to a toothache. When you have a toothache, does anything else seem important? Having a toothache presents a problem very similar to the dilemmas we face in entrepreneurial leadership. A toothache must be dealt with immediately, or it will fester and result in the loss of the tooth, or even serious illness. However, the ultimate solution to the toothache—good dental hygiene—is long-term and not immediate. Similarly, the "hygienic" solution in leadership is creating a common purpose, versus just yanking out people or products.

Practically speaking, the benefits of people working together for a common purpose can be very powerful. In his book *The Functions of the Executive,* noted executive Chester A. Barnard discusses the concept of synergy. According to Barnard, "1 + 1 equals more than 2."[2] His example is simple but enlightening. If five people tried to move a boulder individually, each would move it perhaps a fraction of an inch. However, if five people were working together to move the boulder, they could move it several feet and then some.

Providing this type of direction is critical because having a common purpose can ignite passion. Why? Because when people are passionate about a common purpose, they will *cooperate willingly.*

Inspiring Passion

If a leader wants his or her people to be passionate about a common purpose, that leader needs to incorporate a "win-win" philosophy; that is, "The people win when the organization wins." If a company implements a "win-lose" philosophy, or "winning" at the expense of its people, any sense of a common purpose will quickly be destroyed. It's easy to understand, then, why employees of highly profitable corporations that subsequently announce massive layoffs would be unwilling to cooperate with leaders.

In all three of our turnarounds at Bev-Pak and Adirondack, our people won when we won. However, it was never easy to create passion for our solutions in any of these situations.

* * *

Drawing from our earlier "toothache" example, it would be easy to inspire passion to get rid of the immediate pain but much more difficult to get someone excited about developing the discipline to use good dental hygiene. In difficult situations, the key to keeping people inspired is believing that your long-term solution—a solution based on a solid common purpose—is the best way forward.

Despite the difficulty in all of our turnaround situations, I was thoroughly convinced that we could win if we pulled together. I knew what I wanted Adirondack Beverages to be—the best independent soft drink company in the world—and if we worked together to formulate a plan and execute it, I knew we'd come out on top.

The three turnarounds required me to be honest, sincere, and consistent—the very definition of trust. Most importantly, they required me to lead by example, by living my beliefs and words.

While working as a salesman for Canada Dry, I truly believed we had the best soft drinks in the world. Since Canada Dry supplied our astronauts with drinking water, I'd always explain that our water was "out of this world" (or, at the very least, the best on Earth). After seeing how enthusiastic I was, many of our customers simply called me "Canada Dry." At Adirondack Beverages, it was the same thing: "Here comes Adirondack!" many of my customers and community members would say, knowing full well that my real name was Angelo.

Providing a Process and Creating Coordination

Maintaining a Systematic Process

After creating a common purpose and inspiring passion in that purpose, an entrepreneurial leader must provide, implement, and manage a *systematic process* to accomplish that purpose. Acclaimed quality expert Dr. W. Edwards Deming is the champion of this method and arguably has the best record of success in developing and promoting it. In 1950, he started working with leaders of Japanese industry to help them change their image of poor quality. He is credited with what has been referred to as the miraculous postwar economic recovery and helping Japan to earn a reputation for innovative, high-quality products.

In 1951, to honor Dr. Deming, Japan established the Deming Prize, honoring individuals and organizations that have effectively implemented total quality management. Though he never used this exact term, it has become a popular way of describing his concepts. The Deming Prize is now global and is the most recognized and oldest award of its kind in the world.[3] It is celebrated and broadcast every year nationally on Japanese television.

Upon returning to the United States after his miraculous efforts in Japan, Dr. Deming began a campaign in America to change our method of management. In his book *Out of the Crisis*, he offered "14 Points" that he referred to as the basis for the transformation of American industry. His first and, I believe, most critical point is creating a "constancy of purpose toward improvement of product and service, with the aim to become competitive and to stay in business, and to provide jobs."[4]

Establishing a common purpose without providing a method of accomplishing it is not only useless but also harmful to employees. The civil rights riots of the 1960s, which took place *after* the passage of civil rights legislation, demonstrate what can happen when leaders raise people's hopes and then fail to deliver. In order for leaders to earn credibility, "the process" has to work. In other words, say what you'll do, and then do it. At Adirondack, our new process of employee engagement, as well as benchmarking our efficiency, quality, and service against the best companies in the world, provided energy and enthusiasm to all of us. We were delivering on our promises.

Creating Coordination

Finally, *coordination* is the "strategic alignment" of an organization's people, processes, and assets. This involves acquiring the necessary elements to run the organization and then bringing together the organization's various functions to align with its common purpose.

The best example of strategic alignment that I can provide is how we fixed what I called Adirondack's "quality problem."

Although we had a reputation for outstanding quality, consistently providing quality in all areas was something that we struggled with, as do most organizations. In a great many organizations, the meaning of "quality" is so rarely spelled out. So, our solution was to develop an "operational definition" of quality. We agreed that our operational definition included two elements:

1. Our positioning of the product, and whether it still met our customers' needs.
2. The consistency of our product. Were we meeting the standards that we'd first established? Were we keeping our initial promise to our customers?

We very seldom had a problem with positioning; however, consistency was our nemesis. What we needed was strategic alignment—in other words, we needed to connect our common purpose with the process of making our product. We needed to further align our assets and our people's efforts.

After many failed attempts to fix the problem, we leaders took the issue "to the people." I personally met with employees from every department and shift in our company. In what proved to be very lively discussions among our leaders and employees, the problem became obvious: we couldn't agree on our priorities or standards.

What came out of these discussions was that our leaders were reluctant to stop our processes and make minor corrections, if making the corrections would delay shipping our orders.

"Angelo," they said, "we'll be upset if we short the customer. We want to get our orders out on time!"

Clearly, our very detailed specifications and standards for all products and procedures were losing to "good enough." The employees were frustrated because they were being forced to produce products that, at times, they perceived as being below our standards.

Our solution was to empower every person in the company to stop work if he or she found that a product didn't meet our standards. Salespeople and truck drivers were also permitted to return merchandise for a credit, if they found a faulty product.

At each location in our plant, beginning with the station where materials were received, we posted specific reasons why someone could stop the operation. When an employee stopped the process, he or she had to identify the reason. If an employee found a new reason that wasn't included in our standards, he or she could submit that reason for approval. If a supervisor overrode the employee, then the supervisor had to sign off on this action. These actions were then to be reviewed at our monthly managers' operational meeting, where we would collectively decide who had acted properly. Our main goal was to "do it right the first time."

Each of us took responsibility for our work and passing on acceptable products to the next person in line. This proactive effort dramatically cut down the amount of times that the line had to be stopped. We had a few employee-generated shutdowns, but they were very, very infrequent. Not once did a leader override an operator who'd shut down the process. I'm sure that knowing each incident would be reviewed was a major factor.

To further emphasize the importance of quality, every letter that we received containing a complaint or compliment—we had about a one-to-one ratio—had to be copied and sent to me, along with the manager responsible for answering them. When we developed a response, I would—with my secretary's help—personally send the letter to the consumer. We often contacted the consumer directly. When the company was in its early development stages, I handled these complaints and compliments myself.

It took 18 months to develop our new standards and implement our "stop-work" policy. At the end of the 18 months, a representative from each team presented the standards his or her team had developed at our companywide quarterly meeting. I have to say, it was unbelievable to witness production workers making presentations in front of 180 people with the confidence and expertise of seasoned orators (a difficult task for any of us). I was incredibly impressed with their knowledge and expertise, and I have never been so proud of a group of people in my life.

Professor McGregor, the MIT management professor, was right: people will shine if you give them the opportunity.

Getting Leaders to Cooperate

Coordinating leaders' efforts can be the most difficult step in strategic alignment. I've found that the more pride a leader has in the performance of his or her department, the less he or she is willing to cooperate with other departments. Much too often, leaders wish only for their department to excel, and are reluctant to see other departments outshine theirs. This results in them being reluctant to willingly work with other leaders, since doing so takes away from time they can spend on their own department.

To fix this problem, we made one simple change: we altered our bonus system. At the time, we based our substantial annual bonuses on the following formula: 50 percent was determined by the performance of the manager, and the other half was determined by the performance of the department. Quite frequently, leaders in this position could come close to matching their original salary.

So we decided to change these percentages. We decided that from that point forward, 25 percent of each person's bonus would be determined by a leader's personal performance, 25 percent would be determined by the department's performance, and 50 percent would be determined by the company's performance. From then on, the only way a leader could receive 100 percent of his or her bonus was for the company to be successful. The only way this was going to happen was if managers cooperated with each other.

Interestingly, there was no grumbling or complaining about the new system. I'd thoroughly explained why we were modifying things and why the new system was in all of our best interests. The company had to survive, and in order to be a "world-class" organization, we had to compensate our people fairly. Our leaders inherently understood that, and they could see the benefits of the system immediately. It just so happens that we had our best years after this change, which I don't believe was a coincidence.

* * *

The purpose of a business plan, or any proactive planning, for that matter, is to reduce uncertainty and to get people to cooperate. The more we know about our past performance, as well as the performance of other companies like ourselves, the better chance we have of predicting the future. As we all know, the past isn't a perfect predictor of the future, but it's the best tool we've got. To quote Mark Twain, "The past does not repeat itself, but it rhymes." In the next chapter, we'll explore how proactive leadership earns *credibility*, which forms the core of what I call "personal leadership."

CHAPTER 8

Personal Leadership: Expertise, Trust, Caring, Sharing, and Morality

Five Crucial Questions

Personal leadership can be thought of as the "people" side of leadership. It is the single most important element missing in bureaucracy. Bureaucracy, with its stacks of rules and layers of management, depersonalizes leadership and prevents organizations of all kinds from effectively generating new business.

Through my own experience and independent research, I've found that personal leadership is highly influential in developing strong relationships with co-operators. Leaders must realize that theirs is a position of interdependency, and that they have to be able to build effective relationships, both internally and externally, in order to run a successful company.

As a leader attempts to build a relationship with an employee, that employee will ask five simple questions in assessing whether or not to pursue the relationship. The concepts in these questions—expertise, trust, caring, sharing, and a good moral code—form the core of personal leadership.

1. "Does this leader have expertise in this area?" **Expertise** is the perceived ability and competence of leaders.
2. "Can I trust this leader?" **Trust** is the perceived honesty, sincerity, and dependability of leaders.
3. "Does this leader care about me?" **Caring** is demonstrated through empathy, listening, accessibility, and politeness to employees, regardless of the employee's position in an organization.

4. "Will this leader share with me?" **Sharing** is demonstrated through sharing of authority, information, and rewards.
5. "Does this leader have a strong moral code?" An effective **moral code** is based on generally accepted principles such as treating others the way one would like to be treated, integrity, fairness, and justice.

Only when employees answer each of these questions with a resounding "Yes!" are leaders credible and on the path toward establishing good relationships with their team. We'll take a look at the concept of "credibility" more closely in the coming pages. Now, let's explore each of the elements of personal leadership and what they mean in your journey toward becoming a successful entrepreneurial leader.

Expertise: "Catching Excellence"

I've always loved history, and Abraham Lincoln was and is one of my most admired leaders. I remember a vice president of Canada Dry quoting him once during a motivational presentation, saying, "Anything worth doing is worth doing well." That has always stuck with me. I'm a firm believer that if you're going to do something, you should strive to be the best at it. In other words, as an entrepreneurial leader, you should always try to develop ability and competence, which I call "expertise."

Yet I should emphasize that being the best isn't what matters the most; it is making the effort. It is the *process* that bears the most fruit. As the late, great football coach and motivational speaker Vince Lombardi once said (making this point much better than I ever could), "Perfection is not attainable, but if we chase perfection we can catch excellence."

As CEO of Adirondack Beverages, I always believed that we were a company that pursued excellence long before we instituted our Pursuit of Excellence (POE) program. Yet in dealing with our quality problems—a process during which we clearly couldn't agree on what our standards were—I learned that this wasn't the case.

It took an experience outside of work for me to realize what the solution was. One day, while attending a christening for a friend's son, the minister talked about the Old Testament concept of how "good" was the enemy of "best." Suddenly it dawned on me that our company was guilty of this; "good enough" was often our default standard. The Monday after I heard the sermon, I changed our standard to "best." This was the beginning of our "wow factor" philosophy and our Pursuit of Excellence program. Instead of "good enough," our company would strive for "wows."

We felt this most in the area of change, since we all agreed that we'd no longer make any major changes—including introducing new products—unless the result was the best possible outcome. To determine whether or not we met the wow factor, we'd have people evaluate our ideas on a scale of one to ten, with ten being the highest.

A word about whom we would ask to evaluate our ideas. It is of no value to survey people who are not experts in the area in question (subject matter experts). For example, we would test our taste testers for sensitivity in distinguishing among different flavors and brands. If we knew they were sensitive to Pepsi, for example, and could pick it out from other colas, we would use them to determine if our formula was close in taste to Pepsi's.

When it came to product design, we would use people who did a great deal of shopping for beverages, since they were our target customers. If we were making a change to services and programs, we would survey our customers.

If we couldn't get a "wow" score of nine or ten, we wouldn't make the change. Thankfully, we had a new way to set our standards when it came to products, services, and new programs.

I later learned, while studying for my PhD, that noted economic scholar Herbert Simon won a Nobel Memorial Prize in Economics in 1978 for a theory he called "satisficing": a combination of the words "satisfy" and "suffice." He argued that most people settled for good, not best. Leaders who settle for good instead of being the best can hardly be perceived as having expertise.

Expertise Has to Be Earned

I have found that nothing leads to success like success. In other words, being successful brings with it the perception of expertise. Our perceived expertise by our people, customers, suppliers, and community was based on our track record. The results of our past efforts are still what Adirondack's customers use to judge the company, to this day.

Internal Transparency Builds Trust and Expertise

Each new product or program brings with it a threat to a company's perceived expertise or an opportunity to build upon it. We of course wanted to build upon our internally perceived expertise, so we used the tool of transparency within our company. Internally, we made sure we "sold" our people first by presenting new products at our quarterly meetings.

Our people were always among the first to know about our programs and products.

In meetings where we didn't introduce new products, anxious questions would always follow: "How are we going to grow our business? Do we have any new products that we are introducing?" It wasn't hard to figure out why this was important to our people. Our success would lead to them keeping their jobs, getting overtime, and getting increases in pay. Our failure could cost some of them their overtime and others their jobs.

Transparency was also a big help in selling our POE program to our people. Production, quality, pilferage, and safety results were posted on a regular basis, with improvements earning bonuses for all workers. Sales increases and programs that worked were the best way for us to convince our people that we had expertise.

With customers there were several ways that we established our expertise. One of the best ways was through the grocers' own sales measurement system. The grocers had a system in which they shared sales results of items sold through their warehouses. This system helped them to determine how an item sold through their system compared to other grocers in their competitive area. It also gave them a gauge as to the viability of selling a particular item (they each had minimum limits for carrying items).

Our items were often the top sellers in the Syracuse, New York, market. Our Adirondack Cola was the number-one selling item out of the grocers' warehouses. It even outsold Hellmann's Mayonnaise and Heinz Ketchup.

Articles in newspapers and journals and awards were also very helpful in establishing expertise. The final piece was giving tours of our facility. We had spent over $23 million in capital improvements under our ownership, and the plant had become a showcase. Our facilities had grown to over 400,000 square feet and were filled with modern, high-speed production equipment. When the customers took a tour, it was an instant wow!

Expertise Is Powerful: The OWN Network

In 2011, when OWN (the Oprah Winfrey Network) launched in 80 million homes, it was expected that Oprah would deliver a powerhouse cable network, breathing life into the lagging Discovery Health Channel and its owner, Discovery Communications. So confident was Discovery Communications in Oprah's ability and perceived expertise that it ended up investing more than $500 million in OWN.[1]

It appears that Discovery's confidence in Oprah is paying off. OWN became cash-flow positive in 2013. The first quarter of 2014 was the network's most-watched quarter to date, with double-digit growth across all demographics. OWN now has bragging rights as the fastest-growing cable network among women between the ages of 25 and 54.[2]

Being well known for your expertise in a field is certainly a terrific advantage. In our case, we had beverage consultant John Ritchie to help us out. Mr. Ritchie had come up with Pepsi's original formula and was developing ours. Making a cola formula from scratch is very unusual, and most often it is undertaken by companies like Coca-Cola and PepsiCo, who then distribute the cola to their bottlers. We enjoyed telling our customers about Mr. Ritchie's background—that he'd concocted Pepsi's original formula and was developing ours. I would then show them a cola nut. This was always a hit, since most people, including industry veterans like me, had never seen one up close.

Beware: Perceived Expertise Can Create a False Sense of Trust

Perceived expertise can also swing the other way, as demonstrated by the 2009 Bernie Madoff scandal. Before being arrested and convicted for a $50 billion Ponzi scheme, 70-year-old Madoff was widely considered to have a "magic touch" as an investor, due to his outstanding track record. The *New York Times* reported that he was as an "elder statesman" on Wall Street.[3]

If $50 billion was actually lost, as Madoff apparently claims, this is the largest fraud of this type in history. We can be assured that it wouldn't have been possible had Madoff not been perceived to have expertise, which then led to his being trusted.

Building Trust through Reliability and Quality

I hope that nothing like the Madoff scandal ever touches you or your organization, and that you always focus on building real, lasting trust—the next major component in personal leadership. Trust begins with honesty and sincerity, and ultimately it depends on reliability. Reliability is a matter of being consistent and is an important part of delivering quality.

While studying for my PhD, I found that our definition of quality was similar to that of "quality guru" Joseph Duran, who made many lasting contributions to the field of quality management over more than 70 years. Duran defined quality as "fitness for use," which he then broke down into three parts. "Quality planning" was defining and developing

products to satisfy customer needs; "quality control" was establishing and consistently meeting standards; and "quality improvement"
was based on "proving" the need for improvement and then following
through on remedies.[4]

Our definition was divided in two parts, both based on honesty and
reliability. The first was to position the product properly. This involved
meeting the customer's wants and needs, and communicating our intent
to our customers through honesty in our advertising.

The second part of quality for us was consistently meeting and exceeding our standards. Sadly, this element is often neglected and can lead to
massive recalls and other major problems, as we saw in the auto industry in 2014. Keeping your promise to your customers by consistently
meeting and exceeding your standards is the delivery system for creating
"wows." Consistency also builds trust on a personal level: people who
are consistent can be trusted and therefore are reliable.

Attack the System, Not the People: The 85/15 Rule

When things go wrong in an organization, the best way to build trust is
to attack "the system," not the people. Studies have shown that employees tend to blame the system when things go wrong; however, leaders of
organizations typically blame the people. Who is right? Dr. W. Edwards
Deming claimed that "the system" is wrong 85 percent of the time, and
"the people" are wrong only 15 percent of the time.[5]

One nagging problem we had for years reveals just how true Deming's
axiom is. In food plants, companies consistently fail to keep pallets of
products 18 inches from a wall. Keeping pallets far from the wall enables
companies to clean behind the pallets in order to prevent rodents from
nesting there. Overall, we did very well in keeping our pallets far from
the walls, but it was a constant struggle. Every now and then, we'd be
written up for this issue. Never was it serious enough to warrant failing
an inspection, but we knew that other plants consistently received serious warnings about this issue. An inspector once told us that it was the
number-one infraction for food plants.

We had one manager who was responsible for the location of the pallets. Every time we had a problem, he'd tell me how it was impossible to
get any employees who "cared" about the issue. One day, several years
after his first complaint, he came to me with an idea: perhaps we should
install a metal rail 18 inches off the wall, all around the perimeter of the
storage area. I thought it sounded great, and we gave him the go-ahead.
Immediately after installing the rail, our problem was solved. For the

first time, our forklift operators had a barrier between the wall and the first (back) row of pallets.

Before we installed the rail, it was difficult for our forklift operators to know exactly where to start the back row without constantly getting off the lift and checking. This made things very impractical when a driver was busy and rushed, which was most of the time. Installing the rail eliminated the problem and allowed us to keep the plant cleaner. It also resulted in many compliments from inspectors.

From our experience, we learned that Deming was in fact right: 15 percent of the time, a problem had to do with an employee, and 85 percent of the time, a problem had to do with the system. Most amazing to me was that I visited many other soft drink plants before and after we installed the rail, and never once did I find one that had done the same.

Beware of Performance Appraisals

On a similar note, "attacking the people" through performance appraisals can destroy expertise and trust. In their book *Hard Facts, Dangerous Half-Truths and Total Nonsense*, Stanford professors Jeffrey Pfeffer and Robert Sutton argue,

> Performance rankings can lead to destructive internal competition, which can make it tough to build a culture of knowledge sharing. . . . In addition, there seems to be a self-fulfilling prophecy at work, in which a person who receives a poor evaluation does even worse in the subsequent rating period.[6]

When done right, however, performance appraisals can be a positive factor in any organization. Performance appraisals provide the opportunity for employees to highlight and emphasize their accomplishments, without having their achievements being lumped together with all the others. They allow employees to "break away from the pack," so to speak, and be recognized individually.

I have to be honest and say that I spent years doing performance appraisals, and, like most people, I hated every one of them. During my six years as a sales supervisor at Canada Dry, I would spend two to three days a week working with salespeople for ten hours a day. At the end of each of those shifts, I had to do a performance appraisal noting each salesperson's effort for the day. My promotion to a higher-level management position dramatically reduced the amount of appraisals I had to do; however, it didn't change my strong personal dislike for the process.

The major problem was that we'd been taught in our Canada Dry supervisor training seminars to do two things in our appraisals. We were taught that (1) you had to say something good about the employee, and (2) you had to say something bad about the employee, because no one's perfect and above the need to improve. The first point came back to haunt us when an employee would pull out a previous appraisal where we said something positive. The second point often put us in the uncomfortable position of being critical of our best people.

My solution to this problem was to involve the salespeople in evaluating themselves. In the morning, I'd have each salesperson establish his or her goals for the day. (I helped guide this process by sharing sales figures for the same day and route the previous year.) The salespeople would then have to explain their strategies for achieving their goals. At the end of the day, I'd have them evaluate how they did, against what they'd projected. And then I'd provide my comments.

When I was granted the opportunity and the authority, I implemented this type of appraisal system for our leaders to use among themselves. Our leaders would project their own performance, which, in general, had to be in line with the goals of the organization for the year. If the leaders didn't think they could meet these goals, they'd have to explain why they couldn't uphold their share of the load. If we were dealing with a first-year leader, we'd work together to develop an appraisal, as well as a strategy to meet his or her goals.

Our leaders were allowed to ask for any help that they needed, and to later note whether they were successful in obtaining their request. At the end of the year, leaders were responsible for presenting reports to their supervisors showing how their performances compared with their projections. At that point, leaders were asked to explain why they were successful or not. The leader's immediate supervisor had to sign off on this self-evaluation, and the leader could refuse to sign the appraisal if he or she disagreed with the supervisor's comments. In all cases, I also had to sign off on the appraisal.

Expertise and trust are the building blocks of a relationship between leader and co-operator, but they are of no value unless your people believe that you care about them.

Showing You Care

Who Cares?

Often, when I asked employees if they cared, the following dialogue would ensue:

"Do you care about what happens in this company?" I'd ask.

"Yes!" the employee would respond.

"How about the person next to you?" I'd ask.

"No way do they care!" was always their answer.

"Well," I'd say, "the person next to you says that he cares, but that you don't."

"How about the leaders?" I would then ask.

"No way do they care!"

I suppose it goes without saying that leaders told me that "the people don't care."

The truth is, most people—employees and leaders both—deeply care about their jobs and companies. In many cases, however, people give up trying to show that they care, because they feel no one's listening to them.

Accessibility

One of the most effective methods to prove to your customers and people that you care is through accessibility. This includes being easy to reach and talk to, and being responsive. Employees and customers should be able to reach the person who's the decision maker. There's nothing more frustrating to employees and customers than not being able to get an answer or decision.

Accessibility is also critical when it comes to fellow workers. One of the most frustrating things about working in a bureaucracy is not being able to find someone who will give you a straight answer, help you with a problem, or make a decision. Being there for fellow workers is so important—I had an open-door policy in my office, and everyone was welcome. I also made it a practice to interact with our people at all levels of the company, starting with the janitor, as much as possible.

The importance of interacting with people of all levels was a lesson I'd learned from my first mentor, Carl Touhey. Every time he came to visit me at the plant after being promoted to general manager, we'd take a tour, and he'd stop and talk to every employee. (Of course, he'd ask me their names in advance.) It was striking just how much Carl impressed everyone. For days, I heard snippets of conversations going something like, "The owner stopped to talk to me; he knew my name and asked me how I was doing and how my family was!"

Thanks to Carl, I took frequent tours of the plant, including stopping in on the way home from the movies or going into the plant in the middle of the night, when I'd wake up and not be able to get back to sleep. (Often, my mind would be racing as a result of dealing with everything that ended up on my desk. I never got the "easy" problems; those were solved before they came to me.)

The late-night visits were the best, because I'd get a chance to have coffee and chat with the night shift. The people on night shifts very seldom see the top management of any company, and they were always so impressed and glad when I came. It helped that they also had a chance to tell me how they were doing and pass on some beefs with all of us, including me. The next day, the buzz would be all over the plant, and especially among the managers: "Did you hear that Angelo was here last night? I wonder what's going on?" We took this culture much further by hosting quarterly meetings with all the employees. Everyone was given a voice and the freedom to discuss any subject, without any fear of retribution.

It was also very important for us to stay in touch with the regional managers, who were dispersed over seven states and who were very seldom at headquarters. I visited them frequently and called on customers with them.

Caring through Suggestion

Another effective way to show employees you care is through a "suggestion program," in which employees are permitted to air their thoughts on improvements. Our program required that management provide a detailed response to every suggestion within one week, with explanations for why that response was accepted or rejected. We also awarded prizes to the people who provided beneficial suggestions, and we publicly recognized them in our company newsletter. The authors of the ten best award-winning suggestions (as determined by their peers) were recognized at our annual Christmas party.

By and large, as long as we gave a reasonable explanation, our people would accept our refusal to implement a suggestion. Something as simple and honest as "we can't afford it" was usually more than enough.

Caring about the Customer

It's a terrific advantage to be the CEO of a company, from the perspective of calling on buyers. CEOs are allowed time and leeway in our presentations, unlike salespeople. We get this advantage because buyers are so impressed to see us—usually, CEOs shun sales presentations and linger back at headquarters. My presence at many of these meetings fortified the notion that I cared about the buyer. That notion was further enhanced when I'd see the buyer's CEO and put in a good word for the buyer.

It certainly helped me to be able to "walk a mile" in my customers' and fellow workers' shoes, having been a worker, supervisor, and manager at all levels. The fact that I was raised in modest surroundings, had to work at a very young age, and had to overcome many obstacles and struggles to get ahead also helped a great deal. Perhaps the best lesson of all came from not having been served or waited on as a child, and from always being assigned chores. By doing our chores, my brothers and I learned how to serve and care for others.

Protecting "Them" from "Us"

As absurd as it sounds, one of the best ways I could show my employees and customers I cared was to protect them from us—the management of the company. A CEO, with his or her authority and power, is the most qualified person to do this.

One particular incident stands out in my mind, an incident that shows how I needed to shield customers from "us." I was at my desk one day when one of my managers came charging in, telling me that one of our best customers wanted to purchase 50 truckloads of soft drinks (a $400,000 order), which would be sold over the weekend. The manager was incensed, spouting out how the customer had only given us two days instead of the required three. "The nerve of these people," he said, "wanting the order with no notice! And they want to talk to you, because I told them I didn't think we could do it." By now, I'm sure I don't have to tell you that the customer got the order with my thanks.

In an "ideal" organization, everyone should be willing to serve customers and fellow workers. The organization would also have a CEO who'd know exactly when to protect employees and customers from management. Not only is this an effective way of leading, but it's also an excellent way to convince people that you care about them—but it's not the only way. I find it impossible to believe that people care unless they are also willing to *share*. As we'll discuss in the next section, *rewards* and *recognition* are two of the best ways to share.

The Driver Safety Program: Sharing Our Insurance Savings

In 1982, our insurance agent warned us that Adirondack Beverages wouldn't be able to obtain insurance for our 18-wheelers because of our poor accident rate. He made it clear that he wouldn't be able to find a company that would insure us at any cost. This was a very serious threat to our business—not being able to deliver product would put us out of business.

This was also puzzling to us, since we'd emphasized safety in all our programs and training. We furnished our drivers with the best equipment available, and nearly ideal conditions: all of our drivers went home every night, and no heavy lifting was required. We also paid our drivers above-average wages. Despite all this, we still weren't safe drivers! Something needed to be done.

Our answer was a program that paid our drivers for safe driving, called "The Driver Safety Program," through which we agreed to share our insurance savings with "safe" drivers. We agreed to pay all drivers who didn't have a chargeable accident or moving violation $500 per year; compounded each year by $500, this number would reach $5,000 in the tenth year. We also threw in an all-expenses-paid trip for two to Hawaii—an extra week's vacation for a year—if a driver completed ten years of safe driving.

The accidents stopped immediately. We went on to win safety awards from the states of Massachusetts and New York, and we finished second for a national award.

Why did our program work? Because everyone had the opportunity to win (or lose), no one was pitted against each other, and it was long-term. By offering substantial bonuses for safe driving, and sharing our savings, we raised the consciousness level of our drivers. We also sent the important message that we cared about our drivers' personal welfare.

* * *

Drawing on the success of our driver program, we instituted a similar program with our production and plant employees, offering them 50 percent of what we saved in safety improvements that would reduce our insurance rates. That year we saved $300,000 and added $150,000 to the employee bonus fund. We continued this every year for the next eight years that we owned the company. From what I understand, this program continues to this very day.

Most importantly, our people were working more safely. The total "savings" we accrued were far greater than the monetary rewards to us, seeing that we significantly reduced injuries to our people and reduced lost time due to accidents. Our safety record was so effective that the state of New York recognized us with a special award.

Sharing Recognition

Recognition can be every bit as valuable as financial rewards. Recognizing co-operators by giving credit to deserving people is also the easiest and most inexpensive thing a leader can do. It costs absolutely nothing, and it is free. The only thing I ever took credit for was hiring our people.

We were determined to recognize people in a way that would have lasting effects. After considerable brainstorming discussions, we hit on the answer: we would do it in a way that everyone would be aware of it.

We began by posting signs on equipment recognizing co-operators who had made a significant suggestion that improved its function. The sign would have the improvement and the name of the person who was responsible for it. Visitors would always ask when I gave tours, and it would give me the opportunity to recognize the co-operator. It was also a constant reminder to his or her co-operators.

Around the same time, my marketing assistant, Jack Keller, took it upon himself to design a new sales report. We were taken aback by how effective it was. He streamlined it, making it simpler, with key issues prominently displayed. To recognize him, the report came to be known as the "Keller Report." Each week when it was printed and e-mailed to our regional managers, his name stood out on the top of the report.

The final piece was our annual recognition awards. Our employees would vote on the best suggestions for the year, and the top three would be recognized at our annual Christmas party for all of our people.

* * *

In my career, my personal leadership was based on expertise, trust, caring, and sharing, and it was the basis of how we operated at Adirondack. It is something that is ingrained in my being. When it came time to do my dissertation to complete my PhD, I was determined to test my beliefs.

My dissertation chairperson, James Jaccard, a noted social scientist, agreed to help me develop a questionnaire to measure how effectively leaders practice these four factors: Did they have expertise, were they trustworthy, and did they care and share? How did this affect morale?

With Jim's help I used the questionnaire to measure leadership and morale in 250 different organizations. My two colleagues Erik Eddy, PhD, and Steve Lorentz, PhD, assisted me in publishing the results and findings of my research in the *Leadership and Organizational Development Journal*. We also used the questionnaire in three additional studies and publications, in which we measured leadership and morale in two school districts and a county department of social services.[7]

The questionnaire and studies were a very important part of rounding out my education. I knew that personal leadership was the key to morale and performance, because I practiced it and it worked, but I needed to test it scientifically. With the help of Jim and my colleagues, we found that while professional leadership is a factor in improving morale, personal leadership has the most impact.

We also learned something of real value that we'd missed while developing the theory and questionnaire. In our first study, we were surprised to find that expertise, trust, caring, and sharing explain only 80 percent of personal leadership. In other words, these four characteristics are very important, but there was one characteristic of personal leadership that we hadn't included: moral leadership.

This critically important characteristic is the topic of our next chapter.

CHAPTER 9

Moral Leadership: Dignity, Respect, Fairness, and Morale

Leading by Example

When I first became a supervisor at Adirondack Beverages, my father-in-law sat me down for a serious chat. As food service manager at Binghamton State Hospital, he was used to having several hundred people working underneath him.

"Ange," he said, "when you become a leader, your people will be watching all your actions and listening to every word you say, since what you do and say affects their career and livelihood. They'll be watching you and talking about your every action—mostly the bad ones, since they probably won't even acknowledge the good ones. So, keep these things in mind and act and speak appropriately."

This is arguably one of the main reasons why it is so difficult to lead: whether we choose to or not, we always lead by example. My father-in-law drove this point home to me when I became a supervisor. "Ange," he said, "now your people will be watching everything you do. If you have two alcoholic drinks at a company party, that's what they will be talking about the next day. In the past they would not have paid attention to you or what you did. They will also listen to everything you say now, because you can affect their income and position."

This is also why it is so darn difficult to lead: we are being watched and listened to at all times, and no one is perfect. I have always been aware of this, and I wanted to do more than just lead by example—I wanted our company to *excel* by my example. And I knew that wouldn't happen without a strong moral code.

In his book *The Functions of the Executive*, Chester A. Barnard says that a proper moral code is essential for building and maintaining morale. According to Barnard, the leader of an organization is ultimately responsible for establishing this code:

> Executive positions (a) imply a complex morality, and (b) require a high capacity of responsibility, (c) under conditions of activity, necessitating (d) commensurate general and specific technical abilities as a *moral factor*. These are implicit in the previous discussion; in addition there is required (e) the faculty of *creating* morals for others. It is pertinent now to restate what has already been said, and to amplify and apply it in relation to formal organizations and to the discharge of the executive functions.[1]

I agreed with Barnard's ideas long before I read his book or heard about his philosophy. Simply put, men of weak responsibility can't maintain a moral code, particularly under very complex and dynamic conditions. When all was said and done, setting a moral code at Adirondack fell squarely on my shoulders.

Honoring Dignity, Fostering Respect

To begin my "moral leadership," I made sure to implement two rules in our company when I became CEO and owner. The first, which became our company's motto, was, "Honor each person's dignity and pride." This motto was printed on signs that sat on each leader's desk, and on a banner that hung from the ceiling of the main plant. If I were to create the motto today, I would have added, "regardless of their position or status in life."

The second rule was "Treat others the way you'd like to be treated." This always seemed to be what I call a common-sense rule, because it seemed so logical to me. If I don't like being treated rudely, for instance, then why would I treat someone else this way? There is an old saying that goes, "All good things come to those who wait"; we should add, "All good things come to those who treat others the way they want to be treated."

Fairness through Facts

One of my core beliefs is fairness; however, I found it difficult to put this into practice on a companywide basis. The biggest stumbling block is that fairness is in the eye of the beholder. Fairness the "Adirondack Way" was objective and consistent. I made it clear to our whole team that we would do things the "right way," and not my way or anyone else's, including our leaders'.

The "right way," in order to be objective and consistent, was based on benchmarking ourselves, or comparing our processes and performance to the world's best. Our efficiency ratings for production, for example, would be benchmarked against the industry standard for all major producers, including Pepsi, Coke, and Budweiser. Packaging design was benchmarked against Coca-Cola, and our service levels were benchmarked against Procter & Gamble.

In addition to fairness, this encouraged our people to think outside of the box, versus many companies' fixation on doing things "the way they've always been done." The only rule we attached was that anything would be considered as long as it was ethical, was moral, followed our purpose, and was within our budget for time and money spent.

Dignity through Fairness

We were also fixated on honoring each person's dignity through practicing fairness, even if doing so meant no monetary benefits to management. At Adirondack Beverages, we lived by a decree developed by business leader Mary Parker Follett: the *facts* of a situation, not the people involved, should dictate what's right. (Follett called this the "law of the situation.")

This was one of the most difficult areas for us to master, because people and emotions were always involved. The way we feel toward individuals affects how we deal with them. (I discussed how advantageous it can be when someone likes you in Chapter 5.)

This also applies to how we evaluate them and their conduct. To overcome this, we had a simple rule: when discussing individuals' conduct, we were not allowed to use names. The only person who knew the name was the presenter; all others dealt with the facts of the situation. Key to all of this was that the presenter wasn't allowed to use vague terms like "bad attitude," "lazy," or "not responsible." For example, if an employee wasn't being responsible, the presenter had to provide an incident when a person neglected to perform a certain duty assigned. We had a rule in the Adirondack Way that everything had to be operationally defined.

So often, leaders determine what's "right" simply because they have formal authority. I wasn't going to allow that to be the way we operated— we lived by Follett's decree. I believe a sign should be posted in every workplace saying, "It matters not *who* is right, but *what* is right."

The Dangers of Low Morale

At Canada Dry, I witnessed just how damaging low morale could be. My high spirits and extra effort were rewarded with the wrath of the general manager. The situation robbed me of my energy and willingness to do more than what was expected—so much so that I considered leaving the company shortly after receiving a promotion.

I vowed to never let that happen at Adirondack. Our TQM program began with our quarterly meetings, where everyone in the company had a voice. This lifted morale considerably. Our people were telling me that they thought that this time we just might be "real." We were receiving effective suggestions that were making a difference, and people overall were much more willing to voice their opinions and tell us what they thought about us, our programs, and the company.

It was very important not to disagree with an employee in any way, even if I thought he was wrong. If I were to confront the employee by defending the leader, I could set the program back by months and affect the willingness of our people to speak up.

The Cost of Immorality

What a lot of leaders don't realize is that a good moral code not only fosters morale but also boosts the bottom line. Companies with a good moral code in place typically enjoy good profits and enduring sustainability. Johnson & Johnson is a good example. The following is an abbreviated version of their credo:

- Meeting the needs of all our customers—doctors, nurses, patients, mothers, and fathers—by providing the highest quality products and services.
- Being responsible to each employee by respecting their dignity and recognizing their merit. They must be made to feel secure and compensated fairly.
- Acknowledging our responsibility to the communities we operate in by declaring that we must be good citizens who support good works and charities, and who pay our fair share of taxes.
- Respecting our responsibility to our stockholders whom we owe a sound profit to. We must also invest in research, new ideas, and equipment, and have proper amounts in reserve.

Their final statement is the most impressive to me: "When we operate according to these principles, our stockholders should realize a fair return."[2]

Morality's Powerful Effect

So many of today's business leaders are immoral that employees have come to expect the worst from their bosses. When supervisors act morally, it therefore comes as a surprise and can have a very powerful effect on employees. A good moral code is good for businesses, employees, and all of us in general. It's also beneficial in nontraditional entrepreneurial settings, which I'll discuss in the following chapters.

Part III

ENTREPRENEURIAL LEADERSHIP IN NONPROFITS AND GOVERNMENT

CHAPTER 10

Entrepreneurial Leadership in a Nonprofit Setting

My most effective entrepreneurial venture is a nonprofit called Second Chance, which my wife and I founded in 1987. Second Chance provides deserving students who, for a variety of reasons, didn't attend college immediately after high school with a "second chance" at a college education.

But wait, I hear you saying, *I thought entrepreneurial leadership only applies to businesses!* As I'll discuss in this chapter and the next, this certainly isn't the case. With a few tweaks and modifications, the principles we've learned in both the Opportunity and Enduring Leadership models can be applied to leaders in nonprofits, and—as we'll later learn—even to government as well.

Recognizing Great Opportunity in Humble Beginnings

Like my "real" entrepreneurial venture, Adirondack Beverages, Second Chance began after I recognized an opportunity—an opportunity that I couldn't have seen without my humble beginnings.

I grew up in a modest neighborhood in Endicott, New York, among mostly Italian immigrant families. These were hardworking people who mainly worked at the Endicott Johnson tannery and factories next door—at the time, the largest shoe company in the world. My grandfathers and several of my uncles were some of these employees.

Endicott Johnson had an incentive-based, piecework pay formula. Workers were assigned specific jobs and would "clip" coupons as they completed their tasks. Each coupon amounted to a set amount of money, based on the work performed. Surprisingly, my grandfather Mariano, who used to haul cowhides on his back, loved his job as a leather cutter. I can remember him proudly telling me, "The harder you worked, the more money you made." In 39 years, he never missed a day of work, except for bringing his wife home to Endicott from New York City.

Still, conditions were bad for those who lived near Endicott Johnson. Little attention was paid to the smoke and soot that flowed from the factory's chimneys. Wind would blow black soot our way, covering the clothes hanging on our clothesline. It was a constant struggle for my mother to allow enough time for the clothes to dry on the line before they'd become covered with the awful black dust. Times were tough, and all of us worked together to survive. We all pooled our money to pay the bills, keeping only a modest allowance for ourselves. I myself started working at nine years old, peddling papers.

Several years later, as I watched President John F. Kennedy declare a "war on poverty," I knew that poverty was a problem that needed to be solved. (This was, of course, long before I developed the Opportunity Model.) Yet—as so often happens with opportunities—the problem wasn't quite *ready* to be solved. Presidents Johnson and Nixon poured billions of dollars into the "war on poverty," with little measurable success.[1]

It was only six years later, after I'd bought Adirondack Beverages, that I began to identify a real *solution* to helping beat poverty in my community: giving those in need the chance to attend community college.

I decided to contact the president of our local community college, Hudson Valley Community College, Joe Bulmer, and float my idea by him. After several lengthy, gut-wrenching meetings, we determined that we'd only accept students based on need. Also, we decided we'd provide services, not money, directly to the students. The services included babysitting, transportation, and tutoring. Deciding whom to accept was an extremely difficult process; there were always a lot more students than we could support.

Challenges and Disappointments

The results of our first year of the program were less than impressive; only 19 percent of students had completed the year. I remember sitting at my office desk and reading the report from Hudson Valley, thinking that we'd have to cancel the program. I was very disappointed, and I felt guilty about having wasted so much money on this effort. Several of our friends, including my partner, Al DiPasqua, and the president of Crown Cork & Seal, John Connelly, had given us substantial sums of money—up to $25,000.

As I was getting ready to make the call to cancel the program, I got a phone call from a local attorney.

"Angelo," he said, "I tried to do what you're doing at HVCC but couldn't afford it, so I give one day a week pro bono to help the students at the school. I have two students who've been living together while not married, collecting welfare. They told me that they both received your scholarship and wanted to know if I thought they should get married and give up their welfare checks now that they had this money. Of course the answer was yes, and they got married last Saturday. I thought you should know this."

Wow, I remember thinking, *there is a God*. He heard my frustrations, liked what we were doing, and wanted to make sure I knew that we were on the right track. I also remember thinking that "God helps those who help themselves," so we had to fix our program.

A New Solution

The solution to me was simple: the new program had to be incentive-based. After all, this was how I'd grown up, and it was also how I'd earned much of my pay as a salesman. We changed our awards program to a grade-based system: We'd give $3,000 annually for an A (we have since added a $500 bonus for a perfect 4.0 grade point average (GPA), $2,500 for a B, $2,000 for a C, and nothing for less than a C. Second Chance continued to offer support in terms of tutoring, counseling, and other services provided by our participating schools, but the rest was up to the students.

The impact and results were astonishing. At the end of the first year of our new award system, our completion rate went from 19 to 82 percent with the same pool of students. What's most amazing and rewarding is that the success of our program continues to this day. Today we have five participating schools: Hudson Valley Community College, The College of St. Rose in Albany, New York; Albany University, Broome Community College (now SUNY Broome), and Delhi University. It helps a great deal that all of our schools are now matching our funds. In one case, the school matches in dollars, and in all others they match students. In other words, for every student we sponsor, they match, so we end up supporting twice as many students. To date, with the help of our colleges and universities, we've helped over 1,400 scholars attend college, with grants exceeding $4 million.

Principles for Leading a Successful Nonprofit

So often I hear people say that nonprofits should be more like businesses. I've often thought that businesses should be more like nonprofits. What I've come to believe is that both have best practices that each would benefit from.

A common belief is that there are differences between businesses and nonprofits. What I most often hear is that businesses are profit-driven and nonprofits aren't. I agree with the first statement, but the second statement is far from accurate. Many nonprofits' methods of operation can sure give the impression that their standard is maximizing donations and fundraising.

A good question is whether nonprofits are run differently by their leaders. According to Roger H. Brown, cofounder of Bright Horizons Family Solutions and current president of Berklee College of Music, there is little difference in the management of an enterprise, whether it is for-profit or nonprofit. "It's just a question of who your boss is and who you have to ask for money," he said in a Harvard Business School case study.[2]

The most important and relevant question is, should they be led differently? Are there different principles that we should use for nonprofits? And the answer is absolutely not. I've run both, and I led them exactly the same way.

Understand Surpluses and Deficits

That being said, there are some important differences between for-profit organizations and nonprofits. Foundations have no profits, but there are surpluses and deficits. "Surplus" is just another way of saying profit. Simply put, profit is the difference in what an organization takes in and pays out. And if an organization is taking in less than it is paying out, it is creating losses that can be referred to as deficits.

Deficits are the enemy of surpluses. I have often heard that the answer to creating more surpluses is to incorporate better management practices. Managing funds better is an incomplete solution to the problem; surpluses can best be secured with professional and personal leadership.

I decided from the beginning that we would endow our funds and contributions from others, which would ensure a surplus. With this system, we'd only spend the income from our "fund balance." This would ensure that our program would be sustained in perpetuity, long after my wife and I have left this earth.

Create a Message Using Measurement

Our system worked well, but we soon ran into another problem: we were getting about four to five times the number of applicants that we could support.

In the nonprofit world, "generating new business" means securing donors. I knew it was time for us to start generating new business in a serious way. I decided to begin a campaign to raise money to narrow the gap between new applicants and the "Second Chance Scholars" we were already supporting. We were receiving four to five times as many applicants as we could financially support, and it was time to do something about this.

I also knew we needed a message in order to continue, and that new "business" could only be won by *measurement*. We had to *show* that our program helped make people self-sufficient. In nonprofits, measurement is often "proven" by the number of people helped, and by the amount of money raised.[3] Statistics showing a reduction in a serious problem is also another common method of measurement.[4]

In 2000, we set out to determine the impact of the Second Chance Scholarship Foundation. Through conversations with representatives from participating institutions, interviews with Second Chance Scholars, and a survey of more than 100 Second Chance alumni, we learned that we were having a positive impact: 92 percent of our Scholars graduated from college, and 88 percent were employed. Of those employed, a majority earned more than $20,000 per year.

The results of our measurement efforts were fantastic. They included a six-figure grant from a foundation; a six-figure donation by a local entrepreneur, Marc Newman, to honor his mother; and a seven-figure mention in a will by Warren Hill. Hill, who first read about our program in our local newspaper and has since become a good friend, also started a Second Chance program in his alma mater, Delhi University, and has sponsored several students at SUNY Broome.

Build a Talented Board

For the first eight years of our program, our team consisted of my secretary, Beverly Restina, our lawyer, Jack Clark, and me. By 1995 I no longer owned Adirondack Beverages, and my team, as small it was, no longer existed. I realized that it was time to build a real team for Second Chance, which would involve forming a board and hiring a part-time executive director.

In building a nonprofit board, I relied on the same principles I outlined in Chapter 5. My answer was to surround myself with people whose skills complemented each other's and mine. And yes, character and attitude were the first considerations.

With my recommendation, our board hired Erik Eddy, an old classmate of mine at Albany University, as our executive director. Erik and I had become friends, but more important, I was very impressed with his intelligence, ability to get a job done, and integrity.

With the addition of Erik, we added a professional leader who led the effort to

- Institute and standardize policies on screening applicants;
- Impose spending policies, or limits on what could be spent; and
- Implement timely reporting systems, so we could accurately monitor our scholars' progress.

Unfortunately, as a result of the 2008 stock market collapse, we dissolved our board in 2012. Yet our funds have rebounded due to our savings and the increase in the stock market. With the matching funds from our participating schools, we're currently helping over 80 scholars a year. This number will grow, thanks to winning our most recent battle and raising more funds. Right now, I'm back to overseeing Second Chance and working directly with our participating schools. As they say, "What goes around, comes around."

Stay Focused on the Purpose

Entrepreneurial leaders at both commercial and social enterprises suffer from a very common problem: they lose sight of their larger purpose. As James Austin, Howard Stevenson, and Jane Wei-Skillern tell us in their study *Social and Commercial Entrepreneurship: Same, Different, or Both?*

> In practice, it is often the case that the social entrepreneur becomes increasingly focused on organizational interests as a means to achieve social impact *rather than on social impact itself* [italics added]. . . . The goal of furthering the organization may inadvertently become an end itself, sometimes at the cost of social-value creation.[5]

When it comes to losing sight of an organization's purpose, I've found that the similarities between "commercial" and "social" enterprises are much greater than the differences between the two. In both cases, the purpose of the organization isn't made clear to everyone. At Adirondack we achieved this with our pamphlet that we asked our people to keep at hand and in signs we posted in our facility. Likewise, the purpose of a nonprofit should be posted where it can be seen at all times.

As a reminder, profit, surpluses, equity, or fund balances should never be a goal in either businesses or nonprofits; they are outcomes, as are losses, deficits, and bankruptcy. That being said, in a "social" enterprise, keeping surpluses and fund balances allows you to help more people, and that's always a good situation. Plus no one I know, other than volunteers, is willing to work for free.

Ethics and Morals in Running a Nonprofit

In all nonprofit organizations, the leaders' focus should be on how to achieve the organization's purpose ethically and morally. When done successfully, the organization will have sufficient surpluses and fund balances to grow and prosper.

This can be a challenge, however, in trying economic times. In my case, with the collapse of the stock market in 2008, I was forced to be more "businesslike" with our Second Chance Scholarship program. It soon became clear that I had a choice to make: either I could reduce the number of students we could help, or I could eliminate administration costs.

The one thing that drove my decision was the purpose of the foundation. My wife and I had donated our money to help people become self-sufficient, and our administrative costs were limiting our ability to do this. This was a painful decision, because all the people involved in the administrative side had become personal friends. They'd served for years with no compensation. Oftentimes, they'd sacrificed hours where they could have been earning substantially more.

Once again I faced something very similar to what I'd faced in business many times. The purpose should always be more important than the organization. The organization is only a tool to deliver a purpose. If an organization isn't sustaining itself and can't be turned around, it should be dissolved before it loses its fund balances (equity) and goes bankrupt.

Fortunately our board agreed that helping students was more important then preserving the foundation. A few months later, we held a party, which included our spouses, and reminisced over all the wonderful work we'd done. We were proud to know we'd made a difference and that our efforts would continue.

Know When to Step Back

Second Chance runs very smoothly, thanks to the board's previous contributions and years of refining our program. As a result there's little need to spend a lot of time working with our participating schools, which do all of the administrative work for our program. They also handle all the interaction with students, so we have very limited contact with them, apart from fundraising events and recognition ceremonies.

It's no secret that this is a different leadership experience for me—a person who's used to being involved in every aspect of the organizations I've been responsible for. It leaves me often forgetting about our program and wondering if it works. Yet when I read the reports from our schools and the letters from our students, I'm assured that the program is making a difference. One letter in particular stands out in my mind. It was from the mother of a scholar at Hudson Valley Community College. The scholar, as she said, was a "late bloomer." In his early 40s he became an RN (registered nurse) with the help of our scholarship. As an RN he'd helped many people and had made many friends.

Sadly, our scholar had been diagnosed with cancer, and after a ten-month battle, he passed away. Among his last requests was for his friends to contribute to Second Chance at his alma mater. So far, HVCC has received $2,000 as a result of his request.

* * *

Looking back, there are differences in the needs, strengths, and weaknesses in various types of organizations employing entrepreneurial leaders. Start-ups tend to be very entrepreneurial but lack leadership, including people with management skills. Large companies often have good management skills but lack leadership and are not very entrepreneurial. Nonprofits are much more altruistic but often need to be more entrepreneurial and practice better leadership, including management skills.

In the next chapter, we'll take a look at entrepreneurial leadership in the most unlikely of places: government. And we'll also examine why government needs help in *all* of the aforementioned areas.

CHAPTER 11

Entrepreneurial Leadership
in Government

Government, with its layers of bureaucracy and endless rules, may be thought of as the laughingstock of "serious" entrepreneurs. But it's also one of the most *important* places entrepreneurial leadership can take place. While entrepreneurial leadership admittedly can be difficult in government, it's certainly not impossible.

The simple issue staring the "governmental entrepreneur" in the face is that of control. For a leader to be entrepreneurial, he or she must have control.

In government, "control" most often comes from votes and a leader's relationship with Congress, particularly at higher levels. We'll begin our discussion of entrepreneurial leadership in government with a brief look at three different presidents, all of whom were entrepreneurial leaders in their own right.

Presidential Leadership, Entrepreneurial Spirit: Lincoln, FDR, and Eisenhower

Abraham Lincoln: "The Great Uniter"

When Abraham Lincoln assumed office in 1861, the only way to move goods from one end of the country to the other was by foot or boat. A cross-country trip to the Western states meant a dangerous six-month journey over rivers, deserts, and mountains. The only other options were a hazardous six-week sea voyage around Cape Horn, or going through Central America to cross the Isthmus of Panama by rail.[1]

Lincoln knew the country was never going to grow and prosper under these conditions. He also was well aware of the value of being able to transport goods efficiently. As a young man, Lincoln had worked as a general store assistant in New Salem, Illinois. Part of his duties included piloting a riverboat (which he'd helped to build) down the Sangamon River with surplus bacon, corn, and wheat.[2]

As a former businessman, Lincoln saw an opportunity to connect and secure the nation by uniting it from sea to shining sea. Lincoln knew the opportunity was a problem that was ready to be solved.

To be fair, conversations about a transcontinental railroad first began in the 1830s. But it was Lincoln who passed the Pacific Railroad Act of 1862, which authorized the construction of a transcontinental railway line connecting the Mississippi Valley with the West Coast.

During the following 20 years, industrial production volume, the number of workers employed in industry, and the number of manufacturing plants all more than doubled. From 1890 to 1900, the iron and steel industries went from producing 1,400,000 tons of material to producing 11,000,000 tons. Before the end of the century, America surpassed Great Britain in producing these materials, supplying more than a fourth of the world's supply of pig iron.[3]

Astonishingly, Abraham Lincoln—the mastermind behind our country's "industrial renaissance"—carried out his ideas in the middle of the most costly and devastating war in our history.

Franklin Delano Roosevelt: New Deals, New Hope

Another president who demonstrated exceptional entrepreneurial leadership under extremely challenging circumstances was Franklin Delano Roosevelt, our 32nd president.

FDR was elected president for the first of four terms in November 1932. By March 1933, the unemployment rate had risen to 23.6 percent—nearly one in four Americans was out of work! Thousands of banks had failed between 1929 and 1933, and millions of middle-class Americans had lost their life savings; credit was drying up rapidly. The bank failures had a ripple effect, often taking local businesses with them, which created more job losses.[4]

Across America, circumstances were dire for those of all ages and backgrounds: rural children suffered from rampant disease; 250,000 unemployed teenagers took to freight trains in search of a better life; and African Americans in both the country and cities struggled to find work. Countless farmers were in debt due to considerable financial losses in the 1920s.[5]

On March 4, 1933, FDR told a weary nation, "The only thing we have to fear is fear itself."[6] Millions of desperate listeners tuned in, hoping to have their spirits lifted. Roosevelt was clearly a leader who didn't fear the Depression, the problems it caused, or the presidency.

His adviser, Richard Neustadt, observed, "Roosevelt, almost alone among our Presidents, had no conception of the office to live up to; he was it. His image of the office was himself-in-office. He loved the majesty of the position, relished its powers, and rejoiced in the opportunity it offered for achievement."[7]

According to Neustadt, no other president in the 20th century had a sharper sense of personal power or knew better how to be a master in the White House.[8] Like successful entrepreneurial leaders at commercial enterprises, FDR recognized an opportunity to solve problems for those he served, and he took immediate action. In what became known as the "First Hundred Days," he became the driving force behind Congress passing an incredible 15 bills. He kept his promise to the country of offering a "New Deal."[9] The New Deal was a top-down approach to restore the economy. Under Roosevelt's orders, the government temporarily suspended anti-monopoly laws, and businesses were encouraged to refrain from "cutthroat" competing. Farmers were paid *not* to grow crops, but to help raise prices for future crops.[10] Millions of dollars were pumped into our national infrastructure.

The first New Deal was supposed to restore businesses and farms, but it wasn't working fast enough to increase weak consumer demand. The weak demand was a result of falling wages and millions of workers without jobs.

In 1935 Roosevelt once again demonstrated entrepreneurial leadership and helped pass the Second New Deal, which was a bottom-up approach to restoring the economy. Its aim was to increase demand by funneling energy and funds directly to the people. Using astonishing foresight, Roosevelt implemented several sustainable programs that are still with us today: Social Security, the Federal Deposit Insurance Corporation, and the Securities and Exchange Commission, among others.

FDR's Legacy

Was FDR a great entrepreneurial leader? His impact on the economy remains controversial and debatable. What we do know is that he was aware of the real problems facing his constituents, and that there certainly was a need and demand for his solutions. We know that his actions had an immediate impact, lowering unemployment as he lifted the spirits of the country. For many, he was our most beloved president; when he left us in 1945, the impact was direct and very personal. The following letter to the *Washington Post* from 11-year-old Robert J. Beard captures the nation's sad mood:

> On that Thursday, when I got home from school, both my mom and Nana were crying . . . It was late afternoon, and some people were coming home from work and getting off the bus across the street. Soon I was calling out to them, yelling that Roosevelt had just died. To this day I remember the shocked looks. Some started to cry. Others turned to hurry home, a few running. None said a word back to me . . . But, somehow, they knew I wasn't fooling. Maybe it was because I was crying, too.[11]

Eisenhower: Master of Transportation

President Dwight D. Eisenhower ("Ike"), our 34th president, continued and grew many of FDR's programs. He signed legislation that expanded Social Security, increased the minimum wage, instituted the 40-hour week and created the Department of Health, Education, and Welfare.

Like FDR, Eisenhower was willing to use his power to push through massive programs that would create the conditions to help boost and build the economy for decades to follow. Most notably, Eisenhower signed into law the Federal Aid Highway Act (FAHA) of 1956.[12]

Before FAHA, all that connected our country's cities were poorly maintained one- and two-lane highways.[13] As a young U.S. Army officer, Dwight D. Eisenhower saw firsthand how difficult it was to move goods from place to place. During a cross-country expedition, it took 62 days for his convoy to reach San Francisco from its original destination of Washington, DC.

Yet it took witnessing the efficiency of Germany's autobahns as supreme commander during WWII to compel Ike to action. He was so impressed with the efficiency of the world's first high-speed four-lane highways that he knew he needed to implement a similar system at home. Ike also knew that an effective interstate system would help defend our nation in the event of an emergency, should the Cold War come to U.S. shores.

Lawmakers had been talking about building a highway system for years, and Ike was determined to make it happen. He pushed hard for such a system in his speeches, formal messages, and news conferences. He argued that interstates were essential for the nation's economic development, as well as for national security. Ike's expertise as a military officer and a beloved and trusted leader was certainly a huge advantage in convincing Congress that it was a worthy endeavor.

FAHA provided more than $30 billion for the construction of 41,000 miles of interstate highway. It was, at the time, the largest public construction project in U.S. history. As a result of Ike's action, cities sprang up all across the country along these highway routes, and the U.S. economy boomed—especially the automobile, trucking, and housing industries.

Rising above Bureaucracy

In all our examples above, presidential leaders practiced entrepreneurship long before the concept became popular. These leaders were keenly aware of social problems their "customers" were experiencing. In each example, leaders saw opportunities where others saw problems. Solving these problems was an opportunity for them to serve their people and our country, and an opportunity for each of them to help our country grow and prosper.

Each and every one of these leaders developed unique and special solutions that were profitable and sustainable. We're all still benefiting economically from what they did. All of these special leaders were team players who were able to work with Congress to achieve their goals.

Most significantly, bureaucracy didn't frighten them. To the contrary, they took it head on and were able to rise above its rules and layers of management. They did this, one and all, by seizing control in the form of votes and teamwork with Congress, and through the support of the people who elected them.

Professor Howard Stevenson, the godfather of entrepreneurship studies at Harvard Business School, tells us, "Entrepreneurship is the pursuit of opportunity beyond resources controlled."[14]

The opportunities our presidents pursued and captured were way beyond any resources they controlled—or, for that matter, that anyone controlled. They were able to seize their opportunities and make their programs a reality by harnessing the mass resources of our government. Their gifts would keep on giving for decades and centuries.

Now that's entrepreneurial leadership!

Looking for Today's Leader

Peter Schiff, CEO of Euro Pacific Capital, famously warned of the impending 2008 financial crisis in his 2007 book, *Crash Proof*. He has an even more dire warning for us today: "We've got a much bigger collapse coming, and not just of the markets but of the economy. It's like what you're seeing in Europe right now, only worse."[15] Neil Barofsky, former inspector general of the Troubled Asset Relief Program, agreed:

> We're headed toward another financial crisis, I believe, because we didn't fix the fundamental problems and the perverse incentives and the too-big-to-fail problem that was present in the last one.[16]

The real truth is that the American people need an economy that is generating new business at a rate sufficient to provide good jobs that lead to careers for all those able to work, and for us to pay down our debt. For this to happen, it will take entrepreneurial leadership. Our leaders need only follow the example of our 16th president, "Honest Abe," who had the courage to invest wisely in our future, under the worst possible conditions.

CHAPTER 12

Seven Deadly Leadership Diseases

On my journey chasing and studying leadership perfection, I've found that there are seven deadly leadership diseases endemic to organizations of all kinds: business, nonprofit, and governmental. These are diseases that you won't find on any doctor's list. I developed this list from personal experience, and from observing many entrepreneurial leaders. I offer this list to create awareness and a greater consciousness, and to hopefully help you avoid these diseases' deadly (of course, not literally) grip.

King's/Queen's Disease

King's/Queen's Disease often occurs in people who have been successful and in charge for a long time. In doesn't occur too often in beginners. I certainly didn't have it when I started; in fact, the opposite was true in my case. However, as I learned, it can develop rather quickly if you aren't careful.

It took awhile to turn things around after I bought Adirondack Beverages, but after two years, there was no doubt that we were doing very well. All of a sudden, I noticed that people were treating me differently. Now instead of questioning or criticizing me, they were telling me how wonderful I was. Ironically, many of these people were the same ones who at some point had wondered out loud about my abilities and motives. The good news is that in the past, I didn't believe the bad things they said, so I knew not to believe the good things now.

Yet it would have been easy to fall into the trap of being a "king"—a leader who had all the answers, whose people wouldn't argue with him, and who was treated with considerable reverence by everyone around him. These are the classic symptoms of having King's (Queen's) Disease.

For those of you who feel lulled into being a "king" or "queen," I have some simple words of wisdom:

1. Don't just read your positive press clippings. If you want to really know what's being said about you, read the bad reviews—they're more valuable than the good ones. These reviews may give you an early warning that you're becoming complacent.
2. Surround yourself with people who are better than you at what you do. Then, create an environment where it's healthy to civilly and respectfully disagree. Adopt a policy of "Give me bad news first; good news can always wait," and don't shoot the messenger. The sooner you get bad news, the quicker you can start to work on the solution. The easier and more pleasant you make it for people to be the carriers of bad news, the better the odds will be that you'll get the bad news when it will do you the most good.
3. Finally, create an environment where the focus is on "what's right," not "who is right." Often, if not most of the time, "kings" and "queens" declare and determine *who* is right, rather than *what* is right. Going back to Mary Parker Follett's "law of the situation," the *facts* of the situation should determine what is right and what the solution should be. When it isn't clear which facts are correct, try to rely on credible outside sources that both sides will accept.

Bad Listener Disease

Bad Listener Disease most often follows King's/Queen's Disease, although it can also precede it. Most of the time, it affects successful people and companies. The have-nots—people who are starting out, or companies that aren't yet a factor in the market—most often are great listeners, because they want to learn from those "who have done it."

Listen to the Market

Listening to the market involves seeking an understanding of a situation and proactively responding to threats from competition. This is an essential process for both new and longtime market leaders. Market leaders especially need to be on the alert for threats from competitors, because these leaders have the most to lose. Economist Joseph Schumpeter coined the phrase "creative destruction": attack yourself before your competitor does. When you have the leading product or service in your market, and there's something that can be done to improve it, "listen" to the market and make the improvement before your competitors do. Companies like Procter & Gamble, Gillette, IBM, and Microsoft have done this for years.

The story of the "Bowmar Brain," the first American-made pocket-size electronic calculator, illustrates what happens when companies don't listen to the market. In 1971, Bowmar/Ali Inc. was certainly listening to the marketplace when it attempted to solve problems associated with large, bulky, and expensive calculators—problems ready to be solved. Bowmar's unique solution was the "Bowmar Brain." Soon, Bowmar became one of the largest manufactures of electronic calculators in the world.

Unfortunately, Bowmar forget to be a good listener once it became successful in the marketplace. Known as a technology company after their breakthrough technology, they became reactive rather than proactive. Their competitors, unlike Bowmar, were listening to their customers, who were looking for smaller and less expensive models. Bowmar was unable to react properly, due to large inventories of relatively expensive integrated circuits. In February 1975 Bowmar went bankrupt, leaving behind a legacy of technical and marketing innovations.[1]

Listen to People, Too

Another type of "bad" listening is a failure to listen to individuals on a personal level. "Active" listening is difficult because it's more than being quiet while someone talks—it's not simply a 50-50 effort. Good listening is active listening, a 100 percent effort to fully understand (though not necessarily agree with) the other person.

Asking questions is the first rule of active listening, so that you can make sure you fully understand the meaning of what the other party is saying. Throughout my career I've used two methods of asking questions. The first is to say to the person, "This is what I think I heard you say." Using "think" is very important, because it's not a declaratory statement like, "This is what you said." After telling the person what I *thought* he or she said, word for word, the person would invariably say, "No, I didn't say that."

Don't be surprised when this happens, because most people don't say what they mean on a regular basis. I'll even venture to say that if you recorded what they said and read it back to them, without letting them hear their voices, they'd still insist they didn't say what they actually said.

The second method I used was to try to interpret what I thought the person meant, by saying, "This is what I think I heard you say." I'd then *summarize* what I thought I'd heard. With practice, my bet is that you'll have much better luck guessing what you think the person meant, and that the person will say, "Yes, that is what I said."

You will find, like me, that the second method works better and more often.

Watching for body language will also help you achieve better active listening. It's easy to see when people are agitated and angry—they're usually fidgety and jumpy, and frowning. In these situations I like to say, "I think you're upset. Would you mind telling me why, so that I can understand what's bothering you?"

In his best-selling book *The 7 Habits of Highly Effective People*, author Steve Covey said that striving to understand is one of the most difficult practices, because it requires a change in how we deal with others:

> "Seek first to understand" involves a very deep shift in paradigm. We typically seek first to be understood. Most people don't listen with the intent to understand; they listen with the intent to reply. They're either speaking or preparing to speak. They're filtering everything through their own paradigms, reading their autobiography into other people's lives.[2]

Why is understanding so difficult and important? One answer is that it requires us to put the other person first. I don't have to tell you that this isn't always easy to do. However, it's a great way to convince someone that you care. It's also very beneficial in learning how to deal with and, in the case of employees, lead people of all backgrounds.

Growth for the Sake of Growth Disease

When I attended Harvard's Owner/President Management program, one of our professors told us that we were blinded by the desire to grow. Why? Because all we talked about was growing larger. Growth is very important, but it shouldn't be the focus of leaders. Having a *reason* to grow is much more important.

Growth for the sake of growth often results in the opposite of real growth—a company losing its focus and ending up much smaller, or out of business. In an article for *America's Best*, a magazine for small business owners, Charles Cooper writes,

> Overexpansion is a fairly simple issue and it is a pretty easy trap to avoid, yet thousands of businesses fail each year from falling victim to it. Overexpansion means that you are growing your business too fast, that you have somehow confused success with expansion, and that your business is spinning out of control.[3]

He goes on to say that the signs are easy to recognize—problems with customer service and quality. I would add that another telltale sign is losing key people—often some of your best ones—as a result of the stress of dealing with angry customers.

A great lesson I learned in the OPM program is that no company is entitled to grow—there should always be a good reason. Two of the best reasons are expanding your territory or acquiring unique technology. Another good reason—my favorite—is creating new products and services. This is what I call "earned" growth. Creating new products and services is not the only way to generate new business; continuous improvement of existing products and services will produce new business that is well earned.

When I came back from Harvard, I stepped back and took a long-term focus. I stopped what I called our "Let's Make a Deal" policy and made a conscious effort to think ethically about why we would choose to grow. From that point on, marketing overtook sales, and all deals and promotions had to strengthen our position in the eyes of the consumer.

For two years we slowed down our deal making and price reductions. Despite stagnating in the sales area, our profits doubled by a significant seven-figure amount. Then, just as suddenly, our sales began to soar. By focusing solely on generating new business from creating products and services, and expanding them into markets that needed them, we grew our business 500 percent over thirteen years, an annual growth rate of 39 percent. This despite being in the middle of the "Cola Wars." During this period Coke and Pepsi grew their combined market share from 63.7 percent to 72.2 percent (an 8.5 percent increase), while leading brands 7UP and Royal Crown Cola lost 38 and 53 percent, respectively, of their share of the market.[4] Today only one brand not owned by Coke or Pepsi, Dr. Pepper, is among the top ten best-selling brands.[5]

Spending More Than You Make Disease

Growing too fast often results in cash-flow problems, which, if we're to adhere to our earlier principle that "cash is king," can spell the death knell for a company. To quote Charles Dickens,

> Annual income twenty pounds, annual expenditure nineteen six, result happiness. Annual income twenty pounds, annual expenditure twenty pounds ought and six, result misery.[6]

Harvard professor Phil Thurston once told, in our strategic management class, a story about an immigrant couple in Boston who barely spoke English, and who had a very successful small business, a neighborhood grocery store. When he asked them for "the answer," or their key to success, the husband responded, "Itsa eazie, you godda take in more den you pay out." There are many companies just realizing this lesson.

Millionaires' Disease

After surviving a difficult start at Adirondack Beverages, I found myself doing things simply because we could afford it. Granted, these weren't entirely selfish things, and they were often employee-oriented, but they were still ill-advised. In many cases I found myself saying, "It's only $10,000—we can afford it."

At one point my partner and good friend Al DiPasqua, who'd been my boss at one time at C&C, said, "I remember you when you made decisions based on whether or not it was the right thing to do, not whether you could afford it." He reminded me that in meetings, we often heard, "It's only a million dollars—not a big deal, because we can afford it." This was often said in discussions about buying a larger, better headquarters, or having execs fly first-class. Very seldom were discussions about improving efficiency, service, or employee morale.

When I didn't have the money, I would agonize over whether something was the right thing to do. Of course, where I was going to get the money was the first thing on my mind. As a result, I would do a thorough job investigating the problem, possible solution, and cost.

Surprisingly, when something was the right thing to do at a justifiable cost—in other words, if it was worth the price—I was able to find the money. When you're armed with the facts and a good case, it's amazing how motivated you can be to convince others to loan you money—or front it, in the case of bankers or backers.

Deciding to do something simply because you can afford it bypasses the necessary "homework," and will most often land you on the losing end of the financial equation. Millionaires' Disease is the quickest and easiest way to end up not having the money to do the right thing.

Bottom-Line Blindness Disease

Over the years I've bumped into a very common phenomenon in business that I call "bottom-line blindness": if the bottom line is good, blindness to everything else becomes the norm. Working for both large and small companies, I found that if the profit and loss statement for the month was good, no one asked why it was good, nor did they seem to care. However, when the bottom line was bad—look out! The questions came fast and furious, and you'd better have the answers or find them. Bottom-line blindness often includes a "win at all costs" attitude and culture. In these situations "the ends justify the means," regardless of what's involved in the "ends," or bottom line.

How do we solve bottom-line blindness? We can learn a lot about the solution from former Green Bay Packers coach Vince Lombardi, who openly regretted once saying, "Winning isn't the most important thing; it's the only thing." According to his players and those who knew him well, he was a stickler for the basics. His focus was on fundamentals, discipline, and love—the members of the team had to care about each other. To paraphrase a more obscure saying of his, if you lost a game and are beaten, bloodied, and down on the battlefield, there is no shame in losing, if you gave it your all. The key is a 100 percent effort in doing the right thing.

He went on to say that when you get to be a professional, winning is how you're judged, which makes sense. It also makes sense that you can't win them all, at the professional level and at every other level. The best leaders and people are the ones who have experienced loss and have picked themselves up and gone on to win consistently.

Bottom-line blindness is also a major cause of a very common disease among CEOs, which I call "Attila the Hun Syndrome." In other words, if things are good, and what you did resulted in winning, you could be Attila the Hun and still keep your job. However, if things are bad and you had something to do with it (even if you didn't, but were being offered up as the culprit), you could be Mother Teresa and still be under fire and out the door.

I witnessed this syndrome in both a small company and in the 11th-largest company in the world. In the small company, I knew a general manager who was facing multiple accusations, among them sexual harassment, and complaints from employees that he was diverting funds from our company to his private company. None of these complaints was taken seriously by management. The answer to his accusers always was, "He's making us a lot of money; his division is very profitable."

After years of dodging these issues, he ran into a roadblock. The profits of his division had fallen dramatically, to the point where the division was now a losing proposition. All of a sudden, all the complaints were examined closely, and it was discovered that he had in fact been diverting funds to his personal company.

Ironically, all management could talk about after firing him was all the things that he'd done wrong, forgetting that they had been alerted to them years before.

Greed Disease

The last and most deadly leadership disease is greed for money and power. Greed is most certainly one of the reasons for, and causes of, bottom-line blindness. In many cases Greed Disease occurs behind closed doors, but in the tragic case of Al Lawrence, an insurance entrepreneur from my area, greed was overtly discussed—and glorified.

Lawrence was the owner and CEO of Lawrence Group Inc., a Schenectady, New York-based family of insurance and non-insurance firms. He was also the principal shareholder in Lawrence Insurance Group, a publicly held group of insurance carriers. He built these companies from a one-man agency into one of the area's largest employers.[7]

Mr. Lawrence was well known for his personal generosity. He served on the boards of many nonprofit organizations, and he gave of his money, including $1 million to RPI.

Needless to say, he was one of the New York State Capital District's most prominent citizens. So it was no surprise that he was the keynote breakfast speaker at a half-day seminar for young entrepreneurs in my area in the early 1990s. It so happened that I was also one of the speakers and was seated at the head table during his presentation.

He started off by saying he was just interviewed on the phone that morning by one of our local newspaper reporters regarding the mansion he and his wife had just built. It was a thirty-five-room house with two elevators and eleven bathrooms. They gave the mansion a unique name, LLenroc, which was "Cornell" spelled backward. Drawing on fond memories at college, Lawrence made sure the house was built to look like the building where he'd met his wife. At the time, the house was valued at $19 million.[8]

The reporter asked him if he felt guilty about building such a large house with the increasingly worrisome problem of homelessness in our area. "I couldn't solve the problem," Lawrence told the audience. "The house wasn't big enough to house them all."

He then told the young entrepreneurs about a study conducted at Cornell regarding the factors that led to success. "Do you know what the number-one factor for success is?" he asked. "Greed, and I'm greedy and proud of it."

I was floored! I'd never met Al before, but all I'd heard about him was very positive. I couldn't believe what he was saying to these young entrepreneurs.

Not long after this encounter, Al was brought up on criminal charges. In June 2000, he was convicted of embezzlement and fraud for misusing $37 million that had belonged to employees, policyholders, shareholders, and taxpayers. In one instance, he allowed his publicly held, financially troubled insurance carriers to loan millions to the private agencies, in violation of insurance law. He also was found to have used employee 401(k) retirement contributions to pay the mortgage on the property he owned with his wife.

Lawrence was sentenced to thirty-seven months in federal prison, but he served less than three months. He was released in late November after his cancer was diagnosed as terminal. On January 9, 2002, Al Lawrence died as a result of stomach cancer. His wife was forced to sell their beloved mansion for a fraction of the cost.

In the words of reporter Barbara Pinckney, who spent thirteen years telling the Al Lawrence story, "How sad."

* * *

Ironically, I've learned from experience that these deadly diseases can bring down a leader regardless of his or her stature, power, or wealth. The downfall starts by ignoring your negative press clippings and succumbing to King's/Queen's Disease. It continues by failing to actively listen. Finally, a fixation on growth, money, and power is the least effective method of ending up with them.

Putting morality aside, the best way to end up with money and power is to follow Coach Lombardi's example: focus on the steps required to be successful, rather than developing bottom-line blindness, which can lead to greed.

Part IV

ENDURING RELATIONSHIPS

CHAPTER 13

Relationships That Taught Me to Believe in Myself

I didn't become successful because I climbed on the backs of people around me. I became successful because those people lifted me up.
—Russell Simmons, hip-hop mogul and successful entrepreneur

In Chapter 3, I said that leadership is a process that can be learned. While this is certainly true, leadership most importantly is also a *relationship*: a relationship between leaders and those they lead. Good entrepreneurial leaders will also look to the "outside" relationships in their lives for direction and inspiration when things get tough in their organizations.

Throughout these final chapters, I'd like to share some of the most enduring relationships that I've experienced, and the lessons they taught me on my journey toward becoming a successful entrepreneur. I'll start with relationships that gave me the confidence to begin my first business, Adirondack Beverages.

Relationships That Convinced Me It Was Time to Become an Entrepreneur

I know I must sound like a broken record by now, but I'm going to repeat myself again: the major problem with business and organizations is bureaucracy. When I ended up working for ITT, the 11th-largest company in the world at the time, one of the things we "small company" people quickly learned was that the priorities of many of the managers were very different from ours. Originally we'd been taught that the customer was number one, followed by the company, and then the community. In our new surroundings, the priority list changed dramatically to the following: our résumés (most everyone had their résumé "out there" at all times), what my boss wanted me to say, where my office was, how large my department was, and the company stock price. Nowhere on the list was the customer, the employees, or, for that matter, the company.

Our work was mostly unproductive, which made no sense to those of us who came from small companies. Seventy-five percent of our time was spent in meetings, and writing and answering memos. Often, people would be attacked in memos for breaking some mundane rule, with multiple memo copies sent out to practically everyone in the department.

Most frustrating were the number of senseless meetings and the number of rules, especially in regard to planning.

We were criticized on a regular basis for being too "short-term"—that is, for not being prolific enough in the area of putting long-term planning in writing. To give but one example, I was once asked to submit a five-year business plan in the span of a day.

"Nancy, how can I do this?" I asked a manager at headquarters. I told her that I didn't know the details of the deal I was supposed to write up.

"Ange," she answered, "no one is ever going to read it."

"Oh," I said, "that's easy, then—I'll have it for you after lunch."

It would be unfair not to mention that the company paid us very well and provided good benefits; however, they treated us like objects. Yet mind-boggling bureaucratic incidents were the norm, not the exception. One time, for instance, I was scheduled at the last minute to give a morning presentation the next day in our division headquarters in New Jersey. I ended up not giving the presentation, and sitting in an empty office for close to nine hours, doing next to nothing. Finally, around 4:30 PM, I gave the presentation, thanks to an intervention from my mentor, Al DiPasqua. My regional manager wasn't so lucky. He sat in the lobby all day and left at 5:00, without having had any contact with anyone.

Amazingly, all this made sense to the bureaucrats among us, because the rule was that if anything bad appeared in your file—if you were involved in an assignment or project that failed—there was no way to get ahead. Conversely, if nothing appeared in your file, you were in good shape, so the incentive was to do nothing or as little as possible, and especially never to take a risk.

My headquarters presentation episode convinced me that the best way out of "bureaucracy" was to start my own business, one where I could level the playing field, run a "flat" organization, and make sure that my people could get to the top man or woman. I vowed to give my people a voice someday.

Relationships That Taught Me to Trust My Abilities

After my wife quit work to have our first child, Diane Marie, I realized we would now have to depend on one paycheck. I instantly got the motivation to make the commitment to be successful as a salesman for Canada Dry. The job was the change of direction that I badly needed in my life.

After a lifetime of underachieving, sales finally gave me something that not only could I do well but excel at. I decided that from that point on, I wouldn't quit anything I started without finishing it and excelling in it.

Things went well right off the bat: a few months after starting the job, I surpassed my previous year's earnings, I went on to win a sales contest, and I got to take my wife on a vacation to Bermuda. The numbers proved that I was an outstanding salesman: I had increased my income by 500 percent. This was a building block of my self-esteem. As I was learning, "Nothing builds success like success."

Yet, as with all success stories, I hit a bump in the road—a very big one. I really liked my job, but there was no way I could physically do it long-term. There were days when I'd have to fill grocers' shelves with up to 300 cases of soft drinks—a huge burden when each case weighed 55 pounds. This was partly a result of my success: the harder I worked, the better I was at selling; the more I sold, the harder I'd have to work. Things were approaching the point where it was becoming impossible to do what was required to be successful.

I finally asked for a meeting with my boss to explain my dilemma and ask for help. "Ange," he said when we met, "you're right—it's too much work, and you're my best salesperson. We need a supervisor, and I'm going to contact the higher-ups and tell them I want you in this position." The higher-ups agreed and offered me the job. This was the beginning of my career in leadership, something that I'd never considered.

Solving one dilemma led to a second: I had no idea what a sales supervisor did or what was expected of me. Fortunately I could ask the advice of my father-in-law, Ralph Arnold, who'd been a manager for many years. He was someone for whom I had a great deal of respect. "Ange," he said, "you have to take the job if you don't want to work for a jerk all your life. You see, when you're in management, you get to make the decisions and tell others what to do, rather than have them tell you what to do. The higher up you go, the closer you get to having the final say."

This was all I had to hear—I was tired of being told what to do and was looking forward to leading.

Relationships That Helped Me Buy a Multimillion-Dollar Business with Very Little Money or Formal Education

Al DiPasqua, the executive vice president I reported to at C&C, eventually became my business mentor and close friend. Al had been an entrepreneur and had sold his company to ITT in the seventies. Shortly afterward Al and his partner, Charles Ferro, purchased Bev-Pak, and I was traded like a baseball player to the new company.

At the time that I learned the company was for sale, I contacted Mark Hartman of Crown Cork & Seal, a vice president whom I had known and dealt with for a long time. His company frequently financed purchases of equipment and other companies. Interestingly, if they financed a company, they couldn't force the borrower to buy their equipment or cans, both of which made up the major portion of their business. Their CEO, John Connelly, instituted that policy. Over the years it's been written up in several Harvard Business School cases.

During the process of obtaining Crown's support, Mark cautioned me that Mr. Connelly required a full commitment of my assets.

"Ange, John will ask you to sign over everything you have, or he won't loan you any money," Mark said. "That's his policy."

I then had a phone conversation with John Connelly. When he asked me if I was willing to sign over my assets, I told him, "Mr. Connelly, you can have everything I have if we fail, including the clothes off my back. The only things I won't sign over are my wife and children." This, along with Mark's and Al's endorsements (Mr. Connelly had a tremendous amount of respect for both of them), persuaded John to finance us.

Luckily Al was there to guide me through the purchase of the company. At one point I asked him what the right price was. His answer was a keeper: "It's the price that you can pay back. Don't squabble over money and be penny wise and dollar foolish. If the company can earn enough to pay back what you pay for it, that is the right price." He went on to ask me what my net worth was.

"Ange," he said, "if I pick you up by the ankles and shake you, how much will fall out?"

"Maybe $50,000," was my answer.

"Well," he said, "that's all you can lose, not the millions they're asking for the company."

All along the way, Al asked for and received nothing in return but my respect, thanks, and friendship. He told me, "All I want is to give you a chance to realize your dream." Personally, I used to want to be a football coach or a lawyer, but now, if I'd been given the opportunity to choose any job or career in the world, it would have been to own this company.

It took us 11 months to sign the deal. The process came during the most severe economic conditions business and society had seen in many, many years. We were in the middle of a very serious recession, and interest on working capital peaked at 24.75 percent in 1981. Our first year's interest payment on working capital alone was close to $100,000, and the mortgage was $83,000 a month.

I should add that my wife had to agree to be responsible for half the debt for the rest of her life, even if I divorced her. Amazingly she said okay. She told my mother that she didn't want to stand in the way of me realizing my dreams. This, I believe, is the definition of love. My enduring relationship with my wife gave me something to work for; her love has supported me through thick and thin.

CHAPTER 14

Relationships That Taught Me How to Lead a Business

Without my wife's support, I never would have been able to buy Adirondack Beverages and follow my dream. But I knew better than to cross the line between family and business over the long term. It was a lesson I'd learned back in Endicott.

Friends Are Friends, Business Is Business

After graduating high school and still finding myself living at home, I asked my father to go into business with me. At the time, he worked as a tailor at a men's department store, earning a decent living. He was a terrific tailor but not a very good businessperson. He had learned how to be a tailor by apprenticing in Italy for three years but had never received any training in running a business. I knew I could help bring in new business, as well as manage the business and finances.

I saw an opportunity to be an entrepreneur and work for myself. So I asked my father if he'd like to co-sign on buying a truck. I'd go out and solicit business for him, using skills I'd learned as a paperboy. I didn't know anything about selling, but I was confident I could learn. I'd signed up 60 customers in a month once for the paper, earning myself a trip to New York City.

Unfortunately my mother killed the partnership by refusing to give her blessings to the deal. Seeing that she ran the house—and controlled the finances—she wasn't going to let my father part with a regular paycheck. My father also had all these "paisans"—friends from Italy who owed him money. He'd let them carry a charge account, which unfortunately they never paid. When they owed him too much, they'd just go to the shop up the street, also owned by a fellow paisan, and pay cash. When my father closed down the store, he had shoeboxes full of bills, which he threw in the garbage. "Dad," I said, "what are you doing? Those people owe you a lot of money!" He answered, "Life's too short," and never collected a penny.

Relationships That Taught Me the Value of Hard Work

As I mentioned before, my relationship with work started at a very young age; at nine I was peddling papers for my cousin. At ten I had my own route and at twelve I worked two jobs—one delivering papers, and the second cleaning both a restaurant and a small grocery store. With the exception of an allowance, I gave all the money I earned to my family.

I learned a great deal from working at a young age: how to sell, how to help our family of seven survive, and most importantly, the value of hard work. One of my first difficult jobs was that of a milkman. I reported to work the first day in the dead of winter at 4:00 AM, the latest starting time in my company, in minus-15-degree temperatures. I was shocked to discover that there was no heat in the truck.

Every day I had close to 100 stops to make, 30 of which were third-floor apartments. Running back and forth to the truck to load my milk carrier baskets kept me just warm enough. It was a six-day-a-week job, with every sixth week off with pay (they gave us back our Saturdays). There were no holidays or vacations, just our weeks off.

In addition to this, we were responsible for all the bookwork. It was our job to bill our customers and collect the money. We were responsible for errors in billing—in other words, if what we billed wasn't in line with what the company charged us for the milk (we were allowed $10), the deficit was deducted from our pay. It didn't end there: we were responsible for all bad debts, too. If the customer didn't pay, it was charged to us.

The good news is that I was prepared for this: I had been through it as a paperboy. For six years I worked seven days a week, on sunny, rainy, cold, and snowy days. In that job we were also responsible for billing our customers, collecting the money, and keeping track of bad debts. As it turned out, my ability as a milkman landed me my next opportunity. I earned my second sales job by convincing the sales manager of Canada Dry to become a milk customer.

* * *

When I got to Canada Dry, I was surprised that my selling job required me to stock shelves with soft drinks and to build displays. Done properly, this required very long days, and I'd often return home around 8:00 or 9:00 PM.

The higher up I went, the harder it got, if not physically, then mentally and timewise. As a sales manager and general manager at Bev-Pak, I spent four nights a week on the road for a period of eighteen months, after having just moved my wife and family to Rochester, New York. Later, as a general manager, I put in 60- to 80-hour workweeks.

One of my biggest moral challenges came soon after becoming general manager. I had been given six months to turn the company around, and by the beginning of our summer season, we were making progress. We had the good fortune of the weather warming up quickly, which is always good from the soft drink business's perspective. Plus, some of the new programs we'd developed were starting to work.

Now I faced another problem as a result, and it was the lack of production time: there weren't enough work hours to produce what we were selling. My dilemma is that Carl Touhey had told me that we couldn't run a night shift, which would have doubled our capacity. One night during the previous general manager's tenure, he'd shown up and found production employees on the lawn, playing catch with a football instead of working. As a result, he'd put an end to night shifts.

The pressure was mounting—customers were demanding more product, and we were unable to increase our production. As a person with a strong sales background, refusing to sell product was very frustrating. We had the sales, and I wasn't being allowed to produce the needed soft drinks. In the middle of all this, I was supposed to turn the company around. I remember one day coming back from lunch and having to lie flat on my back on the floor in my office—my head was pounding from answering phone calls from irate customers.

My moral dilemma was that I could solve the problem by adding the night shift, but I would have to deceive Carl to do this. If I didn't, I would jeopardize the future of the company and all the employees' jobs. The way I was brought up with my family values wasn't helping: we didn't lie or deceive; whatever you did, you had to be honest.

I put the night shift on, and our problems were solved. Sales increased along with profits, not to mention the additional jobs that made our employees very happy. Yet not all of my problems were solved—I still had to be careful that no one mentioned the night shift around Carl.

It wasn't long before the charade started to crumble. At lunch one day, Carl looked me in the eye and said, "Ange, are you running a night shift?"

I quickly answered yes—there was no way I was going to lie. I told him I was very sorry to have deceived him, but I couldn't let the company sink and had to do something about it. His response surprised me. "Ange," he said, "I didn't forbid you to run a night shift, I said you 'couldn't' in that you could not make it work. Good job, and thank you."

Relationships That Taught Me Humility

As a supervisor at Canada Dry, one of the real shocks to my system was the realization that this wasn't a "fun" job—quite the opposite. For starters, I lost a substantial amount of income. As a supervisor I was placed on a salary with no incentives, and I ended up with a sizeable reduction in pay.

At twenty-five years old, and with five years at the company, I was the youngest salesperson at Canada Dry, both in age and tenure. Despite my good work ethic, I had no experience in supervision (i.e., acting as a go-between between management and the workforce). This caused quite a bit of resentment by some of my cohorts, who before my promotion had been my friends. At least two of them believed they were more qualified and mature, due to the fact that they had twice as much tenure as I had.

I immediately became a sounding board for all kind of complaints, a situation I wasn't prepared to deal with. From management I'd hear complaints about the salesforce; from the salesforce I'd hear complaints about management. None of these complaints, of course, were delivered directly to either party. Most frustrating were the few incidents where I repeated to either side what the other side had said: never a good idea. Unsurprisingly, the complaints were always promptly denied.

Another big challenge was letting my salespeople "star." I was used to always being either first or second in sales in our company, and now I was expected to take a backseat to my team. This was a real problem for me, because I loved to sell.

Compounding the problem was the fact that I couldn't just sit back and "facilitate" from the sidelines—I had to *show* my salespeople how I'd done what I'd done. And that led to perhaps my most serious problem: I had no idea how to teach how to sell.

Relationships That Taught Me How to Teach My Skills

One of the reasons why I was such a successful salesman was that I was a natural; my weakness was that I had no idea what I was doing or why it worked. Everything I knew about sales was learned by trial and error. It was a very valuable way to learn, but I knew nothing about the basics.

Fortunately, I've always been blessed with the ability to observe successful people and ask for help. One of my first lessons in observing successful people was watching the endless number of Procter & Gamble salespeople calling on customers at the store level.

What struck so many of us salespeople was how structured they were. Oftentimes you'd hear your friends in sales say, "Oh, they're so mechanical—almost like robots." I remember thinking, *Boy, you're right, but they sell a lot of merchandise.* It also dawned on me that they had a structured presentation (we called it a "canned pitch") that they'd make very much the same way to all their customers. The P&G people always had an intro, a body, and a summation. It dawned on me that these were the basics of selling, and we weren't practicing them.

Yet, for as good as the P&G people were, I knew we could improve the process. One of their errors—something that I saw as a basic of good sales—was that they made the same presentation to everyone.

I knew from my city run that plenty of our customers were immigrants who barely spoke English. They were store and bar owners who were battle-weary from growing up and operating in tough neighborhoods. These people were outspoken and liked to test you. Often they'd call me names, laugh, raise their voices, and even yell. They'd love it when I returned the insults: we both knew these were a sign of affection. A "hard sell" came across as an "easy sell" downtown, and it was the only way to make sales.

On the other hand, in my rural territory, it was necessary to start every conversation by asking the buyer how his children were, or how his hobby was going—in other words, to show a genuine interest. Then and only then could you make a presentation. You were never to raise your voice, and you were to make sure that nothing you said or did could be misconstrued as an insult; in other words, you were to avoid at all costs anything that could be perceived to be a "hard sell."

Through both my city and rural relationships, I also learned to add enthusiasm to my canned pitch wherever possible. The key was to begin with an outline of what had to be said—the framework of the deal—and only then to include words and phrases that I believed in and could get excited about. If I believed, for instance, that taste was a factor (i.e., that our product was the best-tasting), I could say this and get excited over it. However, if the product was something I didn't like the taste of, like club soda, I would de-emphasize taste and highlight other factors: that a product was the best-selling club soda, and that the customers loved the taste.

Finally, I learned that all good presentations have a "central theme" and should answer these two questions: "What is the key focus of your presentation? What is the key point you are trying to make to the buyer?" The central theme for our products at Adirondack was our mission—to be "the best value in your beverage section." We also made the effort to define value: "value" was the quality of our products, the quality of our service, and our having the right prices. Our pitching process was easy to remember, because we believed in and were excited about our mission.

Now that I'd learned how I'd done what I'd done as a salesman, I was ready to begin teaching it to my people. I started teaching as a supervisor and continued throughout my career. I believed (and still do) that my first responsibility as a CEO was to teach, and that teaching persuasion was something all our people could benefit from.

Relationships That Taught Me to Have Confidence During a Crisis

I kept getting promoted under Carl Touhey because of my sales success, even though I didn't know the basics of how to sell or why I was successful. Eventually I became the general manager of the company, and I quickly realized that I'd finally found a job I was suited for, one that required a person to be a jack-of-all-trades.

Yet I didn't have much time to bask in my realization, since sales were poor, we were losing a great deal of money, and we'd just laid off half the workforce. Most disturbing to all of us was that the people laid off were, for the most part, very good workers and good people; we just didn't have enough work for them to do. The executive vice president—the same person who recommended me for the job—gave me an ultimatum: "Turn the company around, make it profitable in six months, or the owners will close the plant down."

This might sound boastful or be difficult to believe, but for the first time in my life, I had supreme confidence in my ability to turn the company around. I certainly wasn't familiar with everything that I needed to know, but having an abundance of curiosity and being a quick learner, I didn't believe this was much of a problem. Since I'd taken courses at our local two-year college, Broome Community College, I understood the basics of finance and accounting—key points like break-even, contribution, and how to analyze a P&L sheet. However, the biggest boost to my confidence was that I knew how to sell. My challenge now, along with increasing our actual sales, was to sell our people, starting with the managers, on the idea that we could be winners, working together as a team. I was sure I could do this.

As a sales manager, I'd struggled a lot with direction. I got conflicting directions from my boss (the executive vice president), the president, and the owner. When confronted by my boss, Carl Touhey, as to why sales were bad and not improving, I'd shot back, "When the three of you make up your mind about what you want me to do, then and only then will I have a chance to improve our sales." Carl fixed the problem with one sentence: "Ange, from this day forward, you answer to me and me only." From that day on, sales started to improve.

Shortly after the new understanding with Carl, I was made the general manager. There'd already been two other general managers before me in a very short period of time, and both had failed. They'd run out of candidates, and I was the "What do we have to lose?" choice. The owners figured it couldn't get any worse.

I quickly learned the difference between sales and marketing, a difference that's often not obvious even to professional marketers and salespeople. The marketing manager designs the sales programs, and the salespeople sell them. Marketing involves every area of the company and has to eventually end up with a profit. Salespeople aren't allowed to change the programs that the marketing people design, though they often find ways around this.

For the first time in my career, I didn't have to try to sell programs that I couldn't believe in myself. Also for the first time, I wouldn't have to sell my marketing and sales programs to anyone above me. Although both of these new benefits were huge advantages, the clincher was that I now had the power to implement the programs properly. What a benefit in the area of customer service! I'd no longer have to go through layers of people for us to excel in customer service, or spend a lot of time negotiating with fellow managers or superiors.

Developing Sales Programs, Building Credibility

The first step was to understand what was involved in developing good, solid sales programs. Probably one of the most important lessons I learned about sales was watching a Larry King program late one night. Larry had a guest on who'd written a book on selling, and he asked him what he thought was the most important factor that made a person a successful salesperson.

Before asking this question, Larry had mentioned that 80 percent of all sales are made on the third call, and only 20 percent of salespeople make the third call. Therefore, he concluded, 20 percent of all the salespeople make 80 percent of all the sales.

"Persistence and determination must be number one," Larry said.

The author shot back, loud and clear, "No way, and absolutely not."

The author had done a major study with a large national company. He found that the factor that separated the top 150 salespeople in the company from the bottom 150 was credibility. When the bottom 150 told their customers the cost of a product, the customers didn't believe the product was a good value. However, when the top 150 told their customers the price, they thought that they were getting a bargain.

I have since learned that the most accepted definition of credibility is expertise and trust, both of which lead to believability. I started my own quest for credibility by making sure that I had the expertise to be seen as credible, which I hoped would lead to the reputation of being trustworthy.

I also knew not to exaggerate or stretch the truth, because doing so destroys any possibility of earning credibility in the customer's eyes. This is especially true for repeat sales—customers you call on regularly. "Stretching it a bit" can work on a short-term basis, but word of mouth eventually takes its toll on a salesperson's reputation. Sadly, one-time or infrequent salespeople often never learn this lesson.

I agree with the author that credibility is number one, but let's not overlook the value of persistence and determination and the role they play in being successful. It's even fair to say that some experts believe it's omnipotent:

> Nothing in the world can take the place of persistence. Talent will not; nothing is more common than unsuccessful men with talent. Genius will not; unrewarded genius is almost a proverb. Education will not; the world is full of educated derelicts. Persistence and determination alone are omnipotent. The slogan Press On! has solved and always will solve the problems of the human race.[1]
>
> —Calvin Coolidge

Persistence and determination *are* omnipotent when they're accompanied by credibility. When I was sales manager and general manager at Bev-Pak, I called on a customer for seven years. After doing our regular business, I would pitch him on giving us another region to service. This region was larger than ours and a real plum.

Each time he would say no, and we would both laugh, and I would say, "Okay, but I'm going to keep on bugging you on this." Then one day on my quarterly visit to Chicago, when I tried once again, he said yes. I have to admit I was shocked, but I didn't show it. When I jokingly said, "It's about time," he laughed and told me that he had a serious service problem with his current supplier.

The relationship we'd developed, which was based on mutual respect, along with an impeccable service record, finally paid off. We had established credibility, and thanks to my persistence and never giving up, I walked out the door with $2 million a year of new business.

Relationships That Helped Me to Stay Sincere with Customers

Relationships with customers are the most important element for the survival of any business, and ours was no exception. That's why I was startled to get a call one February day from Al Bregman, the head buyer of P&C Supermarkets. I was the marketing manager for C&C at the time, and I was preparing to buy the company. Al was a good customer, and it was a valuable relationship.

"Ange," Al said, "I'm sorry, but I have to discontinue your company as a supplier for my private label, despite the fact we've been doing business for years and I consider you as a friend." I was in a state of shock, because I would need his business when I bought the company.

"Al," I said, "I'm in the process of buying the company." There was a silence that seemed like an eternity, although it was probably only a minute.

"Are you serious?" he asked. I answered yes.

"Okay, I won't do a thing unless you tell me you couldn't buy it." Al ended up staying a loyal private-label customer and a major supporter of our brands. He went on to tell people that he made our brand for us, and there was a lot of truth to this. Al was Adirondack's first major customer, and he supported the brand with numerous and frequent promotions. He sure was a big help, and it was a great customer relationship.

Relationships That Helped Me Stay Sincere with Suppliers

Staying honest, sincere, and direct with our suppliers was also instrumental to our success. One of our most important relationships was with Crown Cork & Seal, our can supplier and the holder of our mortgage. Mark Hartman, a vice president, and John Connelly, the chairman, were the key players in this relationship. In the spring of 1986, Mark came to visit with news of a major can shortage. He informed me that we'd probably be unable to get cans in the summer, because we weren't a large customer, compared with the major brands of soft drinks and beer. (Along with producing much less volume, we had multiple items—many more than the majors. This increased the cost to Crown Cork & Seal to manufacture our cans.)

"Ange," John told me, "why don't you and Al go see the Old Man?" ("Old Man" was what they called John Connelly.) "The Old Man really likes Al, and I've told him a lot about you. I'm sure he'd like to see you."

I called Mr. Connelly and got through without a wait—amazing, considering he was the CEO of a multibillion-dollar company. When I told John we wanted to visit, he asked why. I said to say hello, period.

When we got to Philadelphia for our visit, we were escorted into his office immediately—again, no wait. John started telling me stories about his neighbor who had the same name as me, along with stories about his family. I took the opportunity to tell him about our foundation, and he promptly gave me a check for $25,000. He said he envied me. I was amazed.

"Mr. Connelly, you created a foundation and donated $130 million to it," I said. "How could you envy me?"

"Angelo," he said, "you get to see the people and their stories and help them. All I do is write checks."

He then settled down to business. "Okay, guys, I've authorized $15 million for you to buy a business, so tell me what it's all about." Crown Cork & Seal, especially under Mr. Connelly's leadership, was well known for providing financing for the purchase of companies. Mr. Connelly was convinced that was the purpose of our visit.

"Mr. Connelly, we don't want to buy anything," I said. "We just wanted to say hello and thank you for your support."

He was genuinely affected, and he had tears in his eyes when he said to his secretary, "Call everyone into the conference room. I want to tell them about Angelo and Al."

The president, vice presidents, and a few others were in the conference room in a matter of minutes. While he was telling them about our company and my foundation, he had tears in his eyes. He gave me a hug so strong that it hurt, which was amazing, considering he was in his late eighties, recovering from a major surgery, and very frail, barely weighing one hundred pounds.

Needless to say, we never went without cans that summer or any other time. What's most significant about this story is that it wasn't in Mr. Connelly's interest, or his business's interest, to supply us with cans that summer. In fact the opposite was true: selling us cans instead of the majors reduced his profits and cost him money. He did what he did because of our relationship. The only regret in this story is something Al expressed in my car on the way back from Philadelphia.

"Ange," he said, "why didn't we go to see the Old Man to just say hello before this?"

"I don't know why," I said, "and I feel guilty that we had ulterior motives."

Relationships That Taught Me How to Deal with Difficult Buyers and People

As you know by now, I began selling at a very young age. After starting as a delivery boy for a tobacco and candy distributor, I went on to become a milkman and later a salesman for Canada Dry. The two latter jobs consisted primarily of pay based on commissions.

It is one of my profound beliefs that every person should, at one time in his or her life, be a salesperson on commission. In this situation, your paycheck is based solely on performance: the better you do, the more you make. Conversely, if you don't sell, there is no paycheck.

What you quickly learn is that being right doesn't matter; what matters is that you make the sale. In other words, as they say, "The customer is always right."

Of course the buyer isn't always right, especially when he or she tries to compromise your integrity. Once, when I was working at Bev-Pak (Adirondack's previous name), a buyer for one of the largest retailers in the country asked me for a bribe, right in front of our broker. He asked that 25 cents a case be paid directly to him. With thousands—possibly millions—of cases being purchased annually, this was no minor issue. I was stunned. Needless to say, we didn't even consider giving him the bribe. When I asked my boss, Carl Touhey, how to deal with the situation, he gave me some of the best advice I've ever received on how to deal with a customer under these circumstances.

"Ange," he said, "don't tell him that this is immoral and wrong, although it most certainly is. You don't want to insult him. Tell him that there's no way you could get this by the comptroller of the company." I took his advice and, most amazingly, never lost the business, despite the buyer never receiving a bribe.

The buyer also isn't right when he or she attacks you personally or is outright unreasonable. As salespeople, we're all faced with these types of buyers.

I remember one such incident when I was badgered by a buyer. He complained about everything from price to service, all of which wasn't justified. Everything I proposed, he belittled. Most irritating is that he seemed to enjoy it.

After swallowing hard several times during my presentation and getting into my car and slamming the steering wheel, I had an epiphany. It dawned on me that this buyer treated everyone the same way, not just me. I'd be justified in my concern if this buyer treated everyone else well, but this simply wasn't the case. *I* wasn't the problem. What I needed to do was change my behavior, and the way I dealt with this type of buyer. From that day forward, I made it my challenge and goal to be able to deal with the most difficult buyers and win them over.

The first thing I had to do was realize that there was very seldom anything personal taking place. There is a "dance" that takes place between a buyer and a seller, and it's usually just business, nothing personal. An excellent example of this was my first call to a major chain in the NYC area. I remember offering the buyer one free case with the purchase of three, a standard introductory offer. He shot back to me that his chain was used to getting two free with the purchase of one. I started laughing. "You must think I'm a hick from the sticks," I said. "I've seen one free with one on very special occasions, but I've never heard of two free with one."

The buyer started laughing, and I soon joined in. The relationship changed because we both knew and understood the rules: it was just business.

Lessons in Good Salesmanship

Eventually we sold the account, and a few years later, while calling on a different buyer for the firm, Joe Gozzi, I was told something startling.

According to Joe, I was the most professional salesman who called on him. I was shocked, because everything I knew, I'd learned from the streets in a rough trial-and-error process. That, and I read everything I could about successful salespeople.

"Joe," I said, "you got to be kidding. This is the biggest market in the country, and companies send their top people to call on you."

"Ange," he said, "you're right—they do. But they think we have to have them, and they take us for granted. So they don't work very hard at selling us. In fact, they're not very professional. The difference is that you work very hard at it and are always prepared."

I wasn't necessarily a great salesman, but I was one of the have-nots. I was hungry—hungry enough to work very hard at it while the "haves" grew complacent.

Another essential element was being prepared. As Vince Lombardi once said, "The lack of preparation makes cowards of us all." This is most important when dealing with difficult people, who tend to be very consistent and do the same thing over and over again. The key is determining *in advance* how you'll respond to them when they're being unreasonable, not when you're in the middle of "battle" and your emotions are frayed.

Another thing to keep in mind is that it *will* seem to get personal at times. These are the times to remember the mantra, "It's just business," even if it seems like you're being individually attacked.

One such incident stands out from my experience at Adirondack. Our contract had expired with a regional chain, and I, along with one of our regional managers, had to call on a vice president to negotiate a new contract for a million cases a year. The buyer yelled and carried on about anything and everything for over three hours. Throughout the ordeal I remained calm and refused to react, until he called me "slick."

"I'm a lot of things," I answered, "but I'm not slick. I'm just an honest man working hard to make a living."

The vice president calmed down and backed off. A short while later, he said, "Ange, you're the only one that didn't raise their voice or get upset during this meeting." (I could see by the pale look on my regional manager's face that he was justifiably shaken up.) I explained that it certainly wouldn't have helped for me to raise my voice, and someone had to be reasonable. We ended up signing the contract.

Driving back to our plant, I had a conversation with our manager, who was still visibly upset. Through my own throbbing headache, I said, "It was a hard day, but we won. We won without selling out our integrity, and I stopped him when he got personal. Most importantly, I had to make a decision when he became obnoxious. I could realize this was business, or I could let my personal ego and feelings get in the way of my business sense. I could personally afford to lose the account, but I would have had to go back to the plant and lay off 14 employees (the number the account supported). I decided that my ego and feelings weren't as important as our employees."

The manager let me know that he understood and that he was glad we were able to keep the business and the jobs for our people.

Lessons in Loyalty

There's something of significance that salespeople often overlook. Specifically, nice buyers are kind to everyone. In other words, they get along with everyone and are easy to sell to. They're also not loyal to anyone in particular, because everyone shares in their business, and your piece is not usually all that large.

Difficult buyers, on the other hand, are much more loyal to the "survivors"—salespeople who have worked very hard to be deemed credible to them and who have earned their trust. Most salespeople give up rather quickly with this type of buyer, and the "survivors" are left to earn most of their business.

The Akel brothers, the previous owners of Giant Markets, a regional chain in my hometown, are a great example. They were some of the toughest, most demanding buyers I have ever dealt with. We would fight over a nickel a case for a couple of weeks, and I would have to overcome many other objections to our programs, in addition to our pricing. Sometimes they even refused to talk to me. They were instrumental in my learning early in my career the value of being prepared and professional. Those who were foolish enough to call on them without being prepared or professional were in for a lively session, and they were never successful. The Akels didn't suffer fools well.

One other key point is that customers can be difficult in different ways, and some difficult ones can be a pleasure to deal with for the most part, as was the case with the Akels. Although tough buyers during negotiations, when the deal was made, they kept every promise and commitment, and they gave our products their full support, which is refreshing in business. Their per-store sales average was the highest of any customer in a seven-state area. They were also very loyal, remaining a customer for over 30 years as well as friends.

On the other hand, we had customers who weren't so difficult to sell to, but who were very difficult after the sale was made. It was always a challenge getting these customers to honor their commitments.

There were also customers, especially some in larger markets, who were difficult because of their practice of deducting non-approved credits when paying invoices. This could amount to thousands of dollars, and it required a great deal of effort to collect. I learned why this practice was so common when I visited a major account in the New York City area. The buyer told me, "Ange, you're one of the few people that even try to collect these deductions. Eighty percent of our vendors never even question them."

Learning That Sales and Entrepreneurial Leadership Have a Common Denominator

Sales, which falls under the umbrella of "entrepreneurial leadership," is totally dependent on the ability to persuade. And being an effective persuader means that you have to be credible, which begins with doing your research. It's critical to know everything possible about a market, including the strengths and weaknesses of competing products and companies, the price structure and service levels of these products, and what's missing in the market.

It's also essential to know who the market leaders are and how they operate. In every industry, companies differ in their marketing strategies. For example, in our industry, grocers generally have two strategies: "high-low" strategies, which offer substantial discounts off the regular pricing, and "everyday low-price" strategies, which offer a steady low price, disregarding deep-discount features.

The clincher is to have proven marketing success. Each time you offer a promotion, a new program, or a new product to a customer and it succeeds, it adds another rung on the credibility ladder. The total package leads to relationships and friendships with buyers in which you'll be able to openly discuss problems and what you can do to solve them. I learned to always start presentations by discussing these issues and telling how we had unique, beneficial solutions to them—better solutions than those of our competitors.

These strong relationships helped to solve our sales problem by generating new business and increasing volume. Within six months—the end of our fiscal year—we were profitable; in fact, we had the best year on record, profit- and sales-wise. We did have some luck—it was extremely hot that summer, which is never a bad thing in the soft-drink industry. But it was the team's hard work that made our success possible. Throughout the year everyone pitched in by working extra hours and taking on additional responsibilities.

After my experience with the first turnaround, we never had to make cuts when facing a loss of sales volume: we'd learned to cut the waste when we were successful, not when times were rough.

Leading this effort was by no means easy; however, it was by far the easiest and most rewarding job I had in sales, supervision, and management up to that point in my career. It also gave me a taste of what it was like to be an entrepreneur (freedom!).

CHAPTER 15

Relationships That Taught Me about Life

We All Can Make a Difference

In 1982, I received a desperate visit from Mark Quandt, the CEO of the Albany Regional Food Bank, a local nonprofit that distributed food to the poor. The Food Bank was just getting started and struggling to survive, distributing about 600,000 pounds a year, which sounds like a large amount. Mark, however, revealed to me that this was nowhere near what they needed to meet the needs of the people in our area.

I was well aware of how difficult conditions were for many Americans. President Reagan had recently asked to reduce a large number of social programs, and this was having an effect on many local families. Nationwide, we were in the midst of a severe recession. Thirteen million American children lived below the poverty line.[1]

The purpose of Mark's visit was to see if we'd sponsor a charity golf tournament. In the process, he made me aware of our local food shortage. As they say, "Out of sight, out of mind." I hadn't encountered hungry people, nor had people with whom I associated. Needless to say, I was in for a good dose of reality.

Mark told me that we were their last resort, because the branded guys refused to help, probably thinking that collecting and distributing food to the poor wasn't "glamorous" enough.

I agreed to help, and I told Mark that raising money from the tournament wasn't the goal. Our goal was to build relationships that would be beneficial to the Food Bank.

At the time, Mark didn't have any serious connections to food companies that might be willing to donate their "mistakes." So I helped Mark reach out to grocers and manufacturers like us that would have mistakes to give to him.

Our company agreed to give the Food Bank "low fills," or cans of soda with less than 12 ounces, the stated amount on the container. Freihofer's Bread Company in Albany gave them bread that was too brown, and local grocers gave them cans with missing labels or with dents.

As for the tournament itself, customers from seven states came to play in it, and we picked up the $30,000 tab. At the post-game dinner, I asked participants to give Mark their "mistakes," and Mark talked about the Food Bank's mission.

The tournament, which is still being sponsored by Adirondack Beverages, was a huge success. It earned the Food Bank $25,000 and led to several significant projects, including a silent auction that raised over $100,000, as well as a Christmas program at a local mall. The Food Bank set up a large Christmas tree, and people's donations were marked by decorations on the tree. Food donations flowed in, and many people also volunteered to serve on Mark's board. The tournament now earns over $100,000 a year, and Mark distributes more than 28 million pounds of food annually.

None of this would have been possible without Mark, his team, and the relationships they built and fostered throughout the years. Our work with the Albany Regional Food Bank is one of the things I'm most proud of, and it's a great example of how relationships lead to success.

Lessons from an Early Leader

My hometown of Endicott, New York, was a village that grew and prospered because of the relationship between an entrepreneurial leader and the people in our community. Mr. George F. Johnson, president and co-owner of Endicott Johnson, the largest shoe company and tannery in the world, has been considered by some to be even more progressive than Henry Ford.

George F. Johnson started life with very little in the way of material resources. Through hard work and intelligence, he became a co-owner and president of Endicott Johnson and a very wealthy man. During the 1920s George and his partner, Henry B. Endicott, turned down an offer to sell their company for $50 million, which in today's dollars would amount to billions. George said he loved what he was doing, his people, and his company, and that he had a lot left to do. George never moved his headquarters, and he stayed in Endicott his whole life.

George lived pretty modestly according to today's CEO standards. He had a very nice house in Endicott, but it was by no means a mansion. George went to church on Sunday with many of his employees. He could also be seen walking the streets of Endicott, greeting people, and letting kids in free in the later innings of Binghamton Triplets games. (The Triplets were a minor-league baseball team that George owned and were part of the New York Yankees farm system.)

George's generosity for his employees and the entire Greater Binghamton area is legendary. He provided free land for many churches, regardless of denomination. He built a hospital that was free of charge for his employees, and whose services were also available at very reasonable costs for everyone in the area. He also gave his employees a free golf course, and built houses for them that were sold with no down payment and no interest charge. He built and maintained all the parks in the area and furnished them with free carousels for everyone. During the Depression years, he provided bread lines and free shoes for local needy people.

Perhaps one of the key lessons of George F. Johnson's leadership is that he never lost his personal touch and contact with his employees. Although EJ, as it was known, was the largest shoe company in the world, it didn't suffer from the problems associated with bureaucracies. George made sure there weren't layers of managers preventing him from maintaining a personal relationship with his employees.

One of the reasons his company thrived and his employees were very satisfied was that each employee's pay was based on incentives. The harder they worked, the more they made. My grandfather Mariano, who was an EJ employee for thirty-nine years, had a picture of George Johnson hanging in the entryway to his house. "Sommer day, Sonny, you gonna be lika dat man," my grandfather liked to say.

Endicott Johnson is no longer in business, but not because of the practices of George F. Johnson. Leadership succession, foreign imports, and unsuccessful mergers took their toll. Greed was never a factor. When I look at the free carousels at the parks, the golf course donated to a city that now houses a senior PGA tour event, the employee hospital, and the many houses Johnson built, I wonder what the area would look like without his having been one of its first and best leaders and entrepreneurs. What would the area where I grew up have looked like if the CEOs of AIG, Goldman Sachs, BP, and most of Wall Street were the business leaders in our community?

Relationships That Taught Me How to Treat Others

My brothers and I were blessed to have a mother and father who didn't have a prejudiced bone in their bodies. We often talked about how we could bring anyone home, regardless of his or her nationality, race, gender, or social standing. My mother insisted that she feed anyone who came into our house, despite the fact that we didn't have a lot monetarily.

However, it wasn't always like this in our neighborhood, which was composed of about 70 percent Italians and 30 percent Slavic people. I'll always remember the day when, as a seven-year-old, I was playing basketball at the park, and a ball went out on the sidewalk. The ball rolled within about five feet of an old woman, who said, "Dirty vop, dirty vop." "Wop" was a very derogatory term for us Italians—the equivalent of the N-word for African Americans.

I couldn't understand, even at my very young age, why this woman—a woman who didn't know me, whom I didn't harm in any way—could hate me so much as to call me this very nasty name. Sadly, the hatred certainly didn't end there. Prejudice toward Italians still exists in some circles. However, I found my early experiences to be a blessing, because I learned what it was like to be hated for no logical reason, just for being different. It gave me a great deal of empathy for all minorities.

Not being prejudiced was also an advantage when it came to hiring at Bev-Pak and Adirondack. When I first started, it was difficult to hire the best people, because they were scooped up by big companies that had a lot to offer, financially and prestige-wise.

I discovered that there was a wealth of talent among older and young people, women, and other minorities. When I left Adirondack, three of our key leaders were women; all of them had started with us at a young age. To quote Veronica Mattas, who in 2014 had been with Adirondack Beverages for 33 years, "I want to give people the opportunity to be listened to, and to show them they can contribute in all kinds of different ways with their jobs."

Relationships That Helped Me Figure Out What to Do Next

I sold my company at age 53 and signed a five-year contract with the purchaser, assuming that my future, at least for a while, was planned out for me. Yet that didn't turn out to be true. First, I encountered some turbulence with the new management: after ten weeks I left by mutual agreement and became a consultant for the firm. Then I was faced with another unexpected problem: my sudden freedom created too many options. Al had warned me about this. Having too many choices can make decisions much more difficult.

Navigating the "Age of Options"

Suddenly being out of work for the first time in 46 years was a shock to my system. I tried overcoming this by exercising my options. It started with golf school with one of the best teachers in the world, David Leadbetter. Six of us then took trips to Spain and Italy, golfing for 100 days straight. None of this solved my problem of what to do next.

Fortunately, shortly after resigning on January 4, 1994, I'd signed up for a two-week program at Harvard for alumni (my executive education program qualified me as an alumnus) called "The Age of Options." It seemed perfect at the time, since it was targeted for people like me—people who had sold their companies, retired at young ages, and were confused about what to do next. I was glad I'd signed up early, because by the time the program started in June, I'd gotten pretty used to doing nothing special. I'd spent a lifetime working hard, with long hours and a lot of stress. Relaxing and doing pretty much anything I wanted to do, within reason (it helped to be financially secure), was starting to feel real good and look pretty attractive.

It was during the Age of Options program that I met Carl Sloane, who ran the program. After a very successful career as cofounder, chairman, and CEO of a large Boston consulting firm, he returned to Harvard, where he had earned an MBA, to become a professor. In addition to our program, he taught leadership and ran another special program with Michael Porter, a world-renowned competitive strategist who developed the classic *The Five Competitive Forces That Shape Strategy* for first-time CEOs of billion-dollar corporations. Sloane finished his tenure at Harvard as the chair of the Human Behavior Department.

For the first time in my life I was forced to use inductive reasoning rather than deductive reasoning. In other words, I wasn't starting with an outcome and deducting how I would get there. Instead I was starting with where I was and identifying where I wanted to end up. After a great deal of work, I discovered that the one thing I hadn't done in my life was to get a formal education. I was the only one of five boys without a college degree. Along with measuring up to my family, I wanted to prove to *myself* that I could follow through on this goal. I'd always told myself that it didn't matter that I didn't have a degree, that I could be successful without it. Well, I'd enjoyed my success and done what I'd had to do—often not what I wanted to do. Now I wanted to try for a degree.

Carl not only made me see the light in terms of advancing my education, but he also became my biggest advocate and supporter.

The next question was what degree to go for. I wanted to earn a PhD, but knew I'd need another degree to pursue one, most likely an advanced degree. So I made a few phone calls; one was to Dianna Stone, a professor at Albany University, who arranged a meeting with Professor Dick Hall, the head of the organizational studies PhD program at Albany. I soon realized that organizational studies was the only PhD program I qualified for, since I'd studied and been a part of several different and diverse organizations, ranging from small to very large.

A salesman at heart, I laid into Dick with my "sales pitch" as to why I should be in the program. Dick quickly cut me off. "Angelo," he said, "you're in!"

An Unexpected Challenge

Dick would let me in, but there were hurdles to clear: to get my doctorate, I'd have to complete sixty-three credits in organizational studies, pass two seven-hour exams in my field and methods/statistics, and write a dissertation. Dick told me he'd contacted Empire College, a work-from-home college in New York State, and that they would give me credit for three years of my bachelor's degree studies based on my past experience. I would then earn the credits necessary for my bachelor's degree by successfully completing one year of the PhD program at Albany University. Incidentally, Dick had also been on a committee that had awarded me an honorary doctorate from SUNY, for the work I'd done with Second Chance and Hudson Valley Community College.

Fortunately I did very well the first semester, and Dick suggested I petition the committee in charge of admission to the doctorate program for acceptance. I did and was accepted. What Dick didn't tell me was that I was basically on my own once I was admitted, and if I wanted help, it was up to me to ask.

This began one of the toughest years of my life. I'd never written an academic paper, and my last math class was Intermediate Algebra, which I'd taken thirty-seven years ago as a junior in high school. Computer literacy was a requirement of the program, and I didn't even know how to turn one on, much less use one!

I eventually decided to hire two tutors: one to help me learn how to use a computer, and one to help with statistics. I worked fourteen hours a day, seven days a week, including Thanksgiving and Easter Sunday. That summer my wife saved my life by buying me a laptop computer and a "Mavis Becon Teaches Typing" tutorial. I played the typing game and practiced all summer; by fall I'd become decent at typing, which also helped a great deal with using the computer. From that point on, I was able to get by working five days a week, although there were still some pretty long hours. With a lot of hard work and help from friends like Erik Eddy, who along with Steve Lorentz coauthored three published papers in *Leadership and Organizational Developmental Journal*, and several professors, I finished my classwork and comprehensive exams in three and a half years. I spent the next two years completing my dissertation and earned a doctorate in the spring of 2000.

I've often said that earning a PhD was the most difficult thing I've ever done in my life. It was certainly harder than the turnarounds I led and harder than running our company. I also have to admit that I didn't even know what a PhD was when I started in the program. Had I known that it would be so focused on theory, and that our program was very quantitative, I most likely wouldn't have attempted earning one. The good news is that it rounded out my education, adding a quantitative and theoretical element to a strong qualitative and empirical perspective. I'd now covered both sides.

Relationships That Taught Me the Importance of Mentoring

Several times in this book I've mentioned just how important and valuable mentors have been for my career and life. I want to reinforce the idea that as a mentor, you have value.

Over the span of my teaching career, I've mentored dozens of students, but two success stories stand out in particular: Arel Moodie and Bert Gervais. These two came into my life at a SIFE (Students in Free Enterprise—now Enactus) meeting, a club I started in 2002 and continue to serve as an adviser for. Knowing I'd been in the beverage business, Arel and Bert approached me after the meeting with an idea for a beverage product.

I suggested that they take my entrepreneurship class, which they did. They proceeded to come up with a new business idea—an online service for college students to find affordable apartments, called Placefinder. com. They went on to win our business plan competition, which was held during the last class of the semester and judged by venture capitalists. Arel and Bert pocketed $5,000 in seed money to start Placefinder. com. Both later served as outstanding presidents of our SIFE club.

They've since sold their company and have gone on to be highly successful motivational speakers. Arel was even named by *Inc.* magazine as one of the "Top 30 Entrepreneurs under 30." He currently hosts the leading iTunes career podcast "The Art of Likability" and runs the College Success Program. His 2009 self-help book, *Your Starting Point for Student Success*, was a best seller. The fact that Arel struggled in a difficult NYC neighborhood growing up makes his success all the more laudable.

Bert, who immigrated here at the age of five from Haiti, also became a best-selling author with his book *Who's in Your Top Hive: Your Guide to Finding Your Success Mentors*. The book shares the lessons he learned during his journey serving as a consultant for major companies like Goldman Sachs. Bert was even acknowledged by President Obama for his work as a young leader in America. Throughout his career Bert's spoken to over 30,000 young adults in 30 states.

What impresses me the most about both of my star students (and I should emphasize that they are *all* stars to me) isn't the success they've achieved but how hard they worked for it and how much they desire to learn—they pick my brains constantly. The sacrifices they've made, and their willingness to give back as mentors themselves to deserving young people, make Bert and Arel shine.

In my own life, my mentors taught me a great deal. Monsignor Brigandi, my spiritual guide, comes to mind, as well as Jim Spano, a name I haven't yet mentioned, who was the sales manager at Canada Dry. Jim helped me learn how to deal with customers and our salesforce. I have Al DiPasqua to thank for both marketing and operation guidance, as well as lessons on how to be a decent human being. All of these people have several things in common: they are all good at what they do and are decent people I admire, respect, and like. Above all, they are the best listeners (besides my wife) I've ever encountered. Not one spent a minute trying to impress me; they were instead always trying to help. When Al helped me buy our company, for example, he told me several times, "All I want is to have the opportunity for you to own the company." His words were genuine.

Mentoring is a selfless endeavor that requires good listening skills, sharing of successes and failures, and the tips you've learned during your journey. My mentees have also taught me a great deal. I learn from their trials and successes. It is energizing and rewarding to see them overcome problems and challenges that hopefully I have assisted with to some degree. I have received as much gratification from helping them as I received from my own mentors.

A Steadfast Mentor, and a Difficult Choice

I would be remiss to conclude my account of this most difficult journey without mentioning Carl Sloane's contribution. Carl gave me the initial confidence to believe that I could earn a PhD. We had several conversations at Harvard, outside the classroom, and he encouraged me to go for it. Unlike Carl, everyone else looked at me like I was crazy, or at the very least way overconfident, when I spoke of my plans to go straight for a PhD and skip two degrees. (Two notable exceptions were my wife, who always amazed me with her full support and confidence in my abilities, and Monsignor Brigandi, who stunned me by saying "of course.")

About 18 months into the PhD program, I became somewhat discouraged with the program's theoretical and quantitative focus. While at an Age of Options reunion, I mentioned this to Carl and told him that I missed Harvard and wished that I could earn my PhD there. Shortly after, he arranged an interview for me with the head of Harvard's PhD program, with his recommendation to accept me.

After a great deal of agonizing, I chose not to take advantage of his efforts. I would have had to forgo 18 months of work that I'd already completed, since Harvard likely would have made me start all over again. The clincher was having to live in Boston, away from my family for three to five years, a sacrifice I wasn't willing to make. In the end, earning a degree at Albany University turned out to be my best option.

Carl's help, however, didn't stop. After I graduated from Albany and was preparing to teach leadership at Binghamton University's MBA program, Carl helped me develop my first two syllabi. He's been a friend and supporter ever since.

Relationships That Taught Me What Really Matters in Life

It took the birth of our third child, Michele Anne ("Shelly"), for me to finally reach maturity at the age of 26. Shelly was born mentally disabled, with several physical disabilities. Among these were an open fontanel (her forehead and the top of her head weren't formed properly), an unusual appearance (a forehead wider then normal, slanted eyes, a pointed nose, and no earlobes), and feet that went completely in opposite directions.

I would be less than honest if I said that Shelly's birth didn't shake the roots of my beliefs, and that it wasn't a severe jolt to both of our systems. Two people deserve a great deal of credit in getting us through this crisis: Doctor Titus Zagakowski, who delivered Shelly and was our family doctor, and—you've heard this before—Monsignor Brigandi. During this time my wife and I were bombarded with well-meaning information and advice, most of it negative.

Doctor Zagakowski was the first voice of reason. "I'm not God," he said. "I can't tell you what's going to happen or what will become of your daughter and what her future will be. My advice is to take it one day at a time and deal with what comes the best you can." I should add that he asked to see her every week and only charged us once a month, knowing we couldn't afford the weekly visit. He was truly concerned about all of us.

My faith was certainly tested by Shelly's condition, and I went to see Monsignor ("Father" at the time) Brigandi.

"Father, this God of ours isn't fair," I said. "Why is he picking on a baby? He should be picking on somebody like me, who can at least fight back, and fight for himself."

"Ange," he said, "you're feeling sorry for yourself. I don't blame you, and I understand. What you have to understand is that your daughter can know a happiness that you'll never experience. She'll be able to get satisfaction out of doing the simplest things, whereas you have to do something challenging to know happiness." He went on to echo the doctor, telling me to take it one day at a time.

Shelly is now forty-eight years old, lives at home with us, and is very happy. I've come to realize that Shelly doesn't have a problem; society does. It is society that decides what's normal and acceptable, and what society decides is arbitrary. Shelly is different and not the same as the "norm"; however, she's acceptable to us and to most people she comes in contact with, with her great sense of humor and "genius" knowledge of popular music. Nor does it matter what others deem acceptable, as long as she has us to take care of her, or someone we choose who can provide proper care. The bottom line is that if we do our job, she'll be very content and live a full and complete life, according to her capabilities. She has everything she needs, and she loves her music and life.

Shelly taught my family the important lessons in life. We have an understanding of the "handicapped" and those who care for them that we may never have had otherwise. The empathy we've gained would never allow us to make fun of anyone not as fortunate as us. We've also learned how precious talent and time is, and not to waste either.

"Feel Sorry for Us"

At a 1992 dinner event for the Amsterdam, New York, chapter of ARC, the National Association of Retarded Citizens, I had the chance to explain why Shelly was as close as I've ever come to having a real hero in my life. There were several hundred people in the room, many of whom were mentally disabled. Speaker after speaker, including administrators from the organization and a local state assemblyman, talked about how unfortunate the "clients" (mentally disabled patients) were. The speakers said we should have sympathy for them and their parents. When it came my turn to speak, I know that I shocked quite a few of the speakers.

"I don't feel sorry for our ARC clients," I said. "I feel sorry for us. Our daughter Shelly can do things that I can't and wish I could. You see, Shelly doesn't know the meaning of prejudice or hate. Yes, my wife will tell you that there are people she doesn't like or is afraid of; however, she'll forgive anyone for anything they've ever done to her, if they just hug her. You see, she loves unconditionally, and I can't do that. Yes—I feel sorry for all of us and not our clients."

After the speech one of the parents came up to me and said, "You know, I've been coming to these dinners for years. I have a special-needs child, and you're the first person who knew what they were talking about."

"Not Everyone Can Be a Social Worker"

Not long after Shelly's birth, I remember having a conversation with Father Brigandi. I was in my early thirties at the time and had just been promoted to general manager at Bev-Pak. Although I'd reached a level of success I couldn't have imagined for myself, I realized I wasn't very happy or satisfied.

"Father," I said, "I don't feel very good about what I'm doing with my life, and I'm not proud of it. I really don't like selling soft drinks—what am I doing besides rotting teeth?"

"Ange, not everyone can be a social worker," he said. "You have responsibilities—a wife and four children, one with special needs. What you *can* do is create an environment for your employees that allows them to grow and prosper. You can also set a good example with your words and deeds. People expect me to say and do good things. That is what priests are supposed to do, and people take it for granted. However, when a businessman says and does good things, people are surprised, because so many are painted in a bad light. This has a very positive effect." Once again, Monsignor Brigandi had nailed it for me.

From my relationships with Monsignor Brigandi, Shelly, and the rest of my family, I've learned that what matters in life is making the most of the gifts and talents that we were given at birth, as well as developing relationships with those who are less fortunate than us. President Obama drove this point home in a speech at Atlanta's Morehouse College in the spring of 2014, when he broke from his prepared remarks:

"Whatever success I have achieved, whatever positions of leadership I have held, depended less on Ivy League degrees or SAT scores or GPAs, and have instead been due to that sense of connection and empathy—the special obligation I felt, as a black man like you, to help those who need it most, people who didn't have the opportunities that I had. Because there but for the grace of God go I. I might have been in their shoes. I might have been in prison. I might have been unemployed. I might not have been able to support a family. And that motivates me."[2]

The president's eloquent words were a reminder for me just how important and valuable relationships are, especially with those who are less fortunate. It goes without saying that whatever success I've enjoyed in my business career didn't depend on degrees or SAT scores or GPAs, since all of my business successes occurred before I had the opportunity to earn a college degree. Whatever success I've enjoyed in both business and life is the result of enduring relationships. It is these "special" relationships, these relationships that lifted me up and carried me my whole life, by the "grace of God," that I wish for everyone. By forging and nurturing these relationships and making use of our special gifts and talents, we *will* make a difference, and we'll feel pretty darn good about life and ourselves when we reach 72.

Conclusion

I enjoyed fairly good success while working for others, but my "real" success as both a businessperson and a human being came through being an entrepreneur. My performance and results were much better because I had the freedom to "do my own thing." I also had the freedom to share my success with people who wanted to learn and who were less fortunate. I never would've found the success, happiness, and self-gratification that I've enjoyed as an entrepreneur had I continued to work for others. Most importantly, my family, students, and many less fortunate people wouldn't have benefited either.

Being an entrepreneur is special because it's good for the human spirit and mind. It provides you with the freedom to think as you please, implement your ideas, and to "do your thing." What a contrast to working for other people and being forced to do things their way! As long as you can pay your mortgage, meet payroll, and maintain happy employees, you're "right." It doesn't matter if someone else thinks you're wrong or that he or she could do it better.

Entrepreneurship has provided me with the freedom and opportunity to be creative in my own ways. I've always wanted to be an artist and to be able to create something special. I can draw and sing, but I've never been able to paint something beautiful or sing a song well enough to earn a living by doing so. Through entrepreneurship, I've been able to create programs and products that people pay their hard-earned money for. I've also created successful companies with workplace environments that allow people to learn, grow, express themselves freely and openly, participate in a cooperative effort, and share in the company's success.

Selling my company gave me the opportunity to return to school, earn my PhD, and become a professor. I love teaching entrepreneurship, because it's "real"—we apply everything we learn to the real world. My students actually create real-life businesses. They pay attention to what I have to say. They work hard in my classes, because they see me as someone who can help make their dream of being an entrepreneur come true.

Looking back, we owe a great deal to many entrepreneurial leaders, whose ideas spawned huge industries. A few of these leaders are Henry Ford, Thomas Edison, Edwin A. Land (cofounder of Polaroid), IBM's Thomas Watson, and Kodak's George Eastman. Many people simply don't realize that entrepreneurs started a great deal of our large and successful companies.

Yet wanting to be an entrepreneur isn't enough. One must also know how to be truly "entrepreneurial"—that is, how to recognize an opportunity, create an organization, bring a product or service to market, and lead effectively. It's the last part that's the biggest challenge for entrepreneurial leaders, but it also represents their greatest opportunity. More than ever before, I have hope that today's entrepreneurial leaders *will* leave a lasting impact on our world.

APPENDIX A

The Pursuit of Excellence

A Lifelong Journey

Summary: The Pursuit of Excellence is a program that is companywide in scope. It is our Total Quality Program geared toward constantly asking ourselves, "How Can We Make It Better?" It is, in fact, a total team effort and requires everyone's commitment to steadily improve. This document outlines specifically what can and will be shared with the employees through their efforts in producing a total quality product and satisfying customer requirements.

I. Goals of the Program

A. To promote the mission of the company

1. To be externally focused versus internally. What is best for our customers, our employees, and our community?
2. To be the best that we can be as a company and as individuals.
3. To be the best value in the beverage industry.

Value = Quality of our products +
Quality of our service +
Right price

B. To live by the morals of the company

1. We believe the most important factors to achieve success are:

TRUST & CREDIBILITY

a. Four keys to building TRUST:
- Honesty
- Preparation
- Responsiveness
- Consistency

b. Three keys to building CREDIBILITY:
- Trust
- Although it is very important to do things right, it is more important to do the right thing
- Proven track record

C. To produce a quality product

D. To maintain a safe working environment

E. To communicate effectively

F. To operate efficiently

G. To reduce waste

II. Calculation of the Kitty

A. Quality Samples – All samples (in-house or from independent labs) tested will be totaled and divided by the number within

Table A.1

Sample % within Standard	Per Case Contribution
Less than 93%	($.005)
93% to 95%	($.0025)
95.1% to 96%	$0.00
96.1% to 98%	$.0025
More than 98%	$.005

standard. Formulation samples will equal 75% of this number and packaging samples 25%.

B. Length of Mistake

The first month we go without a mistake beyond the normal checking period will contribute $100. The second consecutive month will contribute $300. Each consecutive month thereafter will contribute $800.

If there is a mistake beyond the normal checking period, no money will be contributed in that month and the following month will begin again at the $100 level.

C. Customer Complaint Ratio – (Customer complaints divided into production cases)

If the ratio is 9 or lower, $5,000 will be added to the kitty. If the ratio is 10 or greater, $5,000 will be deducted.

D. Efficiencies

Table A.2

Product Size	Efficiency Cases/Hr.	Per Case Contribution	Efficiency Cases/Hr.	Per Case Contribution
12 oz.	1875–1924	$.001	1925	$.002
1.5 L	1300–1399	$.001	1400	$.002
2 L	1450–1524	$.001	1525	$.002
1 L	920–959	$.005	960	$.01
3 L	920–959	$.005	960	$.01
4th Line				
5 L (24 pk)	525–599	$.001	600	$.002
.5 L (12 pk)	850–899	$.005	900	$.001
1 L	725–799	$.001	800	$.002
1.5 L	500–574	$.001	575	$.002
20 oz.	400–474	$.001	475	$.002

When a production record is broken, a contribution of $1 times the number of cases the record is broken by will be made. The minimum contribution will be $100.

E. Warehouse Cases Per Hour

If the ratio of sales to warehouse hours is 480–519, $.0005 per case sold will be added to the kitty. For a ratio of 520 or better, $.00075 per case will be added to the kitty.

F. Misload Program

The first two months without a misload will contribute $100.00 each to the kitty. Each consecutive month thereafter will contribute $300.00

If a misload takes place, no money will be contributed in that month and the following month will begin again at the $100.00 level.

G. Workers Compensation

A calculation will be made annually showing our premium paid versus what our conventional premium would have been. 50% of these savings will be added to the kitty.

In the event our excellent safety record should reverse itself and we are upcharged for workers' compensation insurance, the upcharge in excess of the standard premium will be deducted from the kitty.

H. Total Scrap

This category includes (but is not limited to) raw material scrap and full case losses (low CO_2, Brix full case damages, unexplained inventory shortages).

50% of savings below .008 will be added to the kitty and losses in excess of .0095 will be deducted.

I. Building/Equipment Damages (Due to Abuse or Carelessness)

Every dollar of annual losses in this category under $10,000 will be added to the kitty. Losses over $10,000 will be deducted.

SAMPLE QUARTERLY CALCULATION

Quality samples, efficiencies by line, and warehouse cases per hour are calculated on a quarterly basis.

Below is an example:

Table A.3

Product Size	Actual Cases/Hr.	Production	Production Efficiency	Per Case Contribution
1.5 L	970	100,000	$0.00	$ 0
12 oz.	1,950	1,000,000	$.02	2,000
1 L	980	400,000	$.01	4,000
2 L	1,550	1,000,000	$.002	2,000
3 L	400	475,000	$0.01	4,750
.5 L	400	10,000	$0.00	$ 0
	Total:	2,985,000	$12,750	

Note: The quality sample % is 99%: 2,985,000 × $.005 = $14,925.

Warehouse cases per hour are 570 for the quarter and sales volume was $2,950,000. The addition to the kitty for the quarter would be $2,213 (2,950,000 × .0075).

Misloads and length of mistake calculations are made monthly as explained earlier.

Workers' compensation, scrap, and building/equipment damages calculations are made on an annual basis.

In any year where there is a recall or incident due to an altered product, where any adverse publicity results (i.e., T.V. news), or a public safety hazard is created, there will be no kitty.

In any year where there is a chargeable accident, where loss of an eye, hearing, or limb occurs, or death results, there will be no kitty.

III. Participation in the Kitty

Employees will be awarded either 0 or 1 point per quarter. Employees will receive one (1) bonus point at year end if they receive four quarterly points. Seasonal employees can earn ¾ of a point.

You must be an employee for the full quarter to be eligible for the point.

Below is a chart showing the number of days you need to work to qualify for an accumulation of points:

Table A.4

| | Quarterly Annual Days Worked | | |
8-Hour Shift	9-Hour Shift	10-Hour Shift	Maximum Points
220 or more	196 or more	176 or more	4
165–219	147–195	132–175	3
110–164	98–146	88–131	2
55–109	50–97	44–87	1

If you are injured on the job and no negligence is found, the normal straight-time days lost will be counted as days worked. You will be eligible for the bonus point.

You will not be awarded a point in any quarter when:

1. You are charged with a safety violation or accident.
2. You are suspended.

3. You are issued a written warning (with or without time off). The first written warning, without time off, will result in a loss of one point only (not both the quarterly and bonus point).

IV. Division of the Kitty

At year end (as of December 31), all active (regular, full-time) and summer employees (from the previous summer) will be listed. The points each has earned will be assigned and totaled. The total amount in the kitty will be divided by the total number of points accumulated to arrive at a single-point dollar value. Each employee will then be paid the number of points they have attained times the single-point value.

Example: Kitty Total:........$90,000
              Total Points:............300
              Point Value:...........$300

If you were an employee with 2 points, you would be awarded $600.

V. Other Pertinent Notes:

- Line efficiencies will be reevaluated for new pieces or changes to equipment.

- The Pursuit of Excellence is a lifelong journey and, in fairness to both the company and the employees, is subject to review and change.

- Anyone caught falsifying records/test results will be out of the program for the year and potentially terminated from employment.

- The safety committee will determine whether or not an accident is chargeable.

- WE WILL NOT ALLOW THE QUALITY OF OUR PRODUCTS OR SERVICE TO DECREASE AS A RESULT OF THIS PROGRAM.

VI. Quality Standards (Brix, CO_2, Taste)

Brix   ±0.2   of standard (diets would have negative clinistix)
CO_2 Cans
& plastic   ±0.2   (up to 14 days after production)

plastic only   ±0.2   (15–30 days after production)
                +0.3
                +0.21   (30–60 days after production)
                −0.71
                +0.21   (61–90 days after production)
                −0.91

The above plastic standards are beyond the .3 we over-carbonate to compensate for the .3 loss which occurs within 72 hours after production.

- High readings (±0.5 or less) on low CO_2 items would not be included.

- Taste must meet standard profile for each flavor.

- Packaging—these standards can be found in the Quality Control lab.

APPENDIX B

The Adirondack Way: How Can We Make It Better?

A. Our Mission Statement:

1. To be externally focused versus internally. What is best for our customers, our employees, and our community?

2. To be the best that we can be, as a company and as individuals.

3. To be the best value in the beverage industry.

Value = Quality of our products + Quality of our service + Right price

We believe:

The most important factors for achieving success are:

TRUST & CREDIBILITY

Four Keys to Building TRUST

1. Honesty (our goal is to seek the truth)
2. Preparation
3. Responsiveness
4. Consistency

Three Keys to Building CREDIBLITY
1. Trust

2. A commitment to doing things, and more importantly, doing the right thing
3. Proven track record

B. Adirondack's Three Rules of Operations:

1. Set standards (goals)
   They should be set high, be simple, and be clearly defined
2. Plan your work and work your plan
3. Track the results (control the numbers, not the people)

C. Adirondack's Method of Operation:

1. Please our customers—external and internal
2. Treat others the way you would like to be treated
3. The concept of sharing
4. Empower our people through total involvement and teamwork
5. Four (4) key team-building steps:
   a. Good communication
   b. The basics
   c. Discipline
   d. Caring
6. Three (3) most important steps toward good communications:

LISTEN LISTEN LISTEN

7. Describe (why), demonstrate (how), check, critique (look for good)

8. What do you like? What don't you like? And how would you like to make it better?

9. We support professional and personal growth through education and training for each employee of the company.

10. A focus on developing the questions, to obtain the best results

APPENDIX C

The Enduring Leadership Questionnaire

The following is a questionnaire developed to measure employee morale in all types of organizations. You may find it useful to measure the morale in your own organization, an organization you admire, or an organization that seems to be in trouble.

Leadership Survey

Thank you for agreeing to help us. This survey will ask a wide range of questions about your organization's leadership. We are interested in the behavior of the leadership in your organization, and your attitudes and opinions toward them.

There are no right or wrong answers in this survey. We want only your honest thoughts and feelings so that we can understand employee attitudes toward their leaders. It is very important that you be candid and truthful with us. The scientific integrity of the project depends on it. All of your answers will be held in strict confidence, and the responses you give will be coded into a computer in such a way that it will be impossible to associate you with any of the answers you give. Data will be summarized in terms of average responses for groups of individuals, and at no time will a single person's responses be made public in any way whatsoever. So, please be truthful and candid with us. It is very important.

You will sometimes get the impression that a few of our questions are redundant, that you already answered a very similar question. Please answer all questions, even if you think they are redundant. Sometimes, we need to ask things in slightly different ways, in order for us to get a clear understanding of your thoughts and opinions. So, what may seem redundant to you, may actually be clarifying your opinion to us. Please, bear with us on this. Also, in answering questions, please respond with the first thought that comes into your mind after reading the question. Don't think through every possible aspect of the question as it pertains to your organization. Just give your first honest reaction.

If for any reason you feel uncomfortable answering a question, then just skip it.

Thank you very much for your help with this project!

Survey Terms

This survey uses many terms in a very specific way. It is important that you understand what we mean when we use these terms. The following is a brief explanation of the terms used in the survey. Feel free to rip out this page and have it next to you as you respond to the questions on the following pages.

The Leaders—In organizations, leaders are referred to by many different terms; for example, "leaders," "managers," "executives," "administrators," or "officers." In this survey, the term "the leaders" is used to describe the collective group—all of these leaders in your organization.

Supervisor—This is the person you report to in your organization. These questions refer only to your boss, not all leaders.

Philosophy—The philosophy of an organization can be described as the "strategy" underlying how the organization conducts its affairs. For example, Mercedes-Benz's philosophy is "high quality," L. L. Bean's is "outstanding service," and Walmart's is "the lowest prices."

Programs—Every organization has programs that guide the actions of the employees. Some examples are "the quality program," "the sales program," and "the service program."

Process—Every organization has processes, such as "provide service," "produce products," or even "teach a class."

Rules—These may be rules about many different aspects of the organization—the procedures for "obtaining a day off," "calling in sick," "getting a parking space," "notifying your boss about vacation time," or "leaving work for family affairs."

Mission Statement—This is the purpose for an organization to exist. A university, for example, educates people, and a factory manufactures cars. Examples of mission statements for these organizations would be: "Our university provides the best value in education," and "Our cars are the most economical to run."

Vision—A vision is what your company hopes to achieve. An example of a vision for a car factory would be: "Our goal is to be #1 in our industry (sell the most cars) by the year 2003."

Short-Term Goals—In order to achieve a vision or mission, certain day-to-day tasks must be undertaken, and goals achieved. Examples are "reduce expenses for the quarter," or "improve sales for the month."

Instructions and Example

For each statement below, please indicate the degree to which you agree or disagree by placing the appropriate number next to the statement. We ask that you **answer each question twice**. First, rate the extent that you agree or disagree with the statement with regards to "**the leaders**" of the organization. Next, rate the extent that you agree or disagree with the statement with regards to **your own supervisor**.

1	2	3	4	5
Strongly Disagree	Moderately Disagree	Neither Agree nor Disagree	Moderately Agree	Strongly Agree

Read this statement first →	I cooperate with "the leaders" because I believe their . . .	I cooperate with "my supervisor" because I believe his or her . . .
1. Principles are similar to mine	4	1

In this example, by marking a "4" in the first box, you would **moderately agree** with the statement, "I cooperate with the leaders because I believe their principles are similar to mine." By marking a "1" in the second box, you would **strongly disagree** with the statement, "I cooperate with my supervisor because I believe his or her principles are similar to mine."

Please note that, from time to time, the response alternative scale may change. We note this in the survey when it happens.

Professional Leadership—Providing Direction

For each statement below, please use the following scale:

1	2	3	4	5
Almost Never	Sometimes	A Moderate Amount	Quite Often	Almost All the Time

Read this statement first →	"The leaders" explain . . .	My supervisor explains . . .
1. Our organization's mission		
2. Our organization's vision		
3. Our organization's philosophy		
4. Why attaining the vision is important to the success of our organization		
5. Why our philosophy is designed to be in the best interests of the employees		
6. How the employees will benefit if the organization is successful		
7. Why attaining the vision is in the best interest of the employees		

Professional Leadership—Providing Process

Read this statement first →	"The leaders" explain . . .	My supervisor explains . . .
8. How our programs are designed to attain the organization's vision		
9. How our processes are designed to maintain the organization's mission		
10. How our programs are designed to improve customer satisfaction		
11. How our processes incorporate our organization's philosophy		

Professional Leadership—Providing Coordination

Read this statement first →	"The leaders" explain . . .	My supervisor explains . . .
12. How my job contributes to the vision		
13. How our department contributes to attaining the vision		
14. Why maintaining our organization's mission is in the best interest of the employees		
15. Why attaining success for our organization is in the best interest of the employees		

Personal Leadership—Expertise

For each statement below, please use the following scale:

1	2	3	4	5
Almost Never	Sometimes	A Moderate Amount	Quite Often	Almost All the Time

Read this statement first →	"The leaders" are . . .	My supervisor is . . .
16. Able to make programs work		
17. Doing a good job of creating cooperation between departments		
18. Demonstrating considerable skill at work		
19. Worthy of praise based on performance		
20. Thoroughly prepared before acting		

Personal Leadership—Trust

Read this statement first →	"The leaders" are . . .	My supervisor is . . .
21. Sincere when working		
22. Honest at work		
23. Consistently doing what they say they will do		
24. Consistently doing what they say they will do when they say they will do it		
25. Behaving in a manner consistent with past actions on similar issues		

Personal Leadership—Caring

Read this statement first →	"The leaders" . . .	My supervisor . . .
26. Make(s) every effort to understand us in our daily dialogue		
27. Make(s) every effort to understand what is meant when discussing important issues		
28. Make(s) it easy for employees to make suggestions		
29. Respect(s) the rights of employees		
30. Deal(s) with employees politely regardless of the employee's position		
31. Make(s) every opportunity for advancement available to us		

Personal Leadership—Sharing

For each statement below, please use the following scale:

1	2	3	4	5
Almost Never	Sometimes	A Moderate Amount	Quite Often	Almost All the Time

Read this statement first →	"The leaders" . . .	My supervisor . . .
32. Share(s) recognition with us		
33. Allow(s) employees to be part of establishing objectives		
34. Allow(s) employees to be a part of improving our processes		
35. Share(s) authority willingly		
36. Share(s) knowledge with us		

Personal Leadership—Acting Morally

For each statement below, please use the following scale:

1	2	3	4	5
Strongly Disagree	Moderately Disagree	Neither Agree nor Disagree	Moderately Agree	Strongly Agree

Read this statement first →	"The leaders" . . .	My supervisor . . .
37. Always allow(s) employees to present their side of the story		
38. Always act(s) justly when there is a problem		
39. Always act(s) fairly		
40. Focus(es) on doing the "right thing"		
41. Have (has) very high principles		

Morale/Willing Cooperation

For each statement below, please use the following scale:

1	2	3	4	5
Strongly Disagree	Moderately Disagree	Neither Agree nor Disagree	Moderately Agree	Strongly Agree

Read this statement first →	I cooperate with "the leaders" because I believe their . . .	I cooperate with "my supervisor" because I believe his or her . . .
42. Principles are similar to mine		
43. Vision for the future is positive		
44. Mission for our organization is positive		
45. Programs are strong		
Read this statement first →	I cooperate with "the leaders" because I am excited about . . .	I cooperate with "my supervisor" because I am excited about . . .
46. The vision for our company		
47. Performance of our organization		

Demographics

Please tell us about yourself by answering the following questions.

1. What is your age (in years)?

2. Gender: _____ Male _____ Female

3. Race:

   _____ Caucasian   _____ African American

   _____ Asian or Asian American _____ Hispanic American

   _____ Native American   _____ Other

4. Are you a United States citizen?   _____ Yes _____ No

5. What is your country of birth?_____

6. How many years of full-time work experience do you have?_____

7. What is your current job title? _____

8. Are you a member of "the leadership" (as described in the questionnaire?

   _____ Yes _____ No

If you answered yes to Question 8, please check the line that best describes your position (check only one line).

_____ Supervisory Level _____ Middle Level _____ Executive Level

9. How long have been in your current position (in years)?

10. How many years of college do you have (in years)?

11. Do you have any college degrees?   Yes   No

   If the answer to Question 11 is yes, please list the type of degrees.

_____

Note: This is a clinical copy that provides headings above each group of questions that informs the reader of what it is attempting to measure. For example, on page 186 the heading is: **Professional Leadership— Providing Direction.** This type of heading appears before each category and should be deleted when applying the questionnaire.

Notes

Prologue

1. *The Men Who Built America*, episode no. 107: "When One Ends, Another Begins." The History Channel, 2012.

2. "The Jeff Bezos School of Long-Term Thinking," 99U.com (accessed February 11, 2015), http://99u.com/articles/7255/the-jeff-bezos -school-of-long-term-thinking.

3. Joseph A. Schumpeter, *The Theory of Economic Development: An Inquiry into Profits, Capital, Credit, Interest, and the Business Cycle (Social Science Classics Series)* (Transaction Publishers, 1982).

4. Joseph Y. Calhoun, "What Is Entrepreneurship? Steve Jobs and Herman Cain Define It," *Thinking Things Over* 1, no. 12 (October 2008).

5. W. B. Gartner, "'Who Is an Entrepreneur?' Is the Wrong Question," *American Journal of Small Business* 12, no. 4, 26 and 11–32.

6. Candida Brush, "Practicing Entrepreneurship: Creation and Creativity," *Forbes*, October 23, 2014.

7. Drew Hendricks, "10 Companies Revolutionizing Entrepreneurship," *Forbes*, September 4, 2014.

8. Peter F. Drucker, *Innovation and Entrepreneurship* (New York: HarperBusiness, 2006), 143.

9. Ibid.

10. "An Entrepreneurial Generation of 18- to 34-Year-Olds Wants to Start Companies When Economy Rebounds, According to New Poll," Ewing Marion Kauffman Foundation (accessed February 2, 2015), http:// www.kauffman.org/newsroom/2012/11/an-entrepreneurial-generation -of-18-to-34yearolds-wants-to-start-companies-when-economy-rebounds -according-to-new-poll.

Chapter 1

1. "Niche Marketing Definition," *Entrepreneur* online encyclopedia (accessed February 2, 2015), http://www.entrepreneur.com/encyclopedia/niche-marketing.

2. "Market Saturation Definition," Businessdictionary.com (accessed February 2, 2015), http://www.businessdictionary.com/definition/market-saturation.html.

3. "The Auto Industry, 1920–1929," Bryant University website (accessed February 2, 2015), http://web.bryant.edu/~ehu/h364/materials/cars/cars%20_30.htm.

4. Henry Ford, *My Life and Work* (Standard Publications, Inc., 2006).

5. Jay Yarrow, "Steve Ballmer's Huge Reorg of Microsoft Could Bury One of the Company's Biggest Embarassments," SAI section, *Business Insider*, July 9, 2013.

6. Jessica Lee, "Bing Grows Search Market Share—at Yahoo's Expense, Not Google's," Searchenginewatch.com, last modified July 17, 2013 (accessed July 17, 2013), http://searchenginewatch.com/sew/news/2283151/bing-grows-search-market-share-at-yahoos-expense-not-googles#.

7. "Automobile in American Life and Society," University of Michigan—Dearborn and Benson Ford Research Center website (accessed February 2, 2015), http://www.autolife.umd.umich.edu.

8. Hannah Elliott, "Luxury Car Sales Stronger Than Ever: Rolls-Royce Has Another Record-Breaking Year," *Forbes*, January 9, 2014.

9. "Primary Demand Definition," Businessdictionary.com (accessed February 2, 2015), http://www.businessdictionary.com/definition/primary-demand.html.

10. U.S. Department of Transportation, Office of the Assistant Secretary for Research and Technology (accessed February 11, 2015), http://www.rita.dot.gov.

11. "Citibike: How It Works," Citibike website (accessed February 2, 2015), http://www.citibikenyc.com/how-it-works.

12. David Lester, "Business Ideas That Changed the World: The Walkman," startups.co.uk, March 16, 2015 (accessed August 10, 2015), http://startups.co.uk/business-ideas-that-changed-the-world-the-walkman/.

13. Peter F. Drucker, *Innovation and Entrepreneurship* (New York: HarperBusiness, 2006).

14. "Virtusphere Product Description," Virtusphere website (accessed February 2, 2015), http://www.virtusphere.com/Product.html.

15. Al Ries and Jack Trout, *Marketing Warfare* (New York: McGraw-Hill, 1997).

16. "Adult Obesity Facts," Centers for Disease Control and Prevention website (accessed February 2, 2015), http://www.cdc.gov/obesity/data/adult.html.

17. Jessica Todd and Rosanna Mentzer Morrison, "Less Eating Out, Improved Diets, and More Family Meals in the Wake of the Great Recession," USDA Economic Research Service website (accessed February 22, 2015), http://ers.usda.gov/amber-waves/2014-march/less-eating-out,-improved-diets,-and-more-family-meals-in-the-wake-of-the-great-recession.

18. "The FAGE Story," Fage company website (accessed February 2, 2015), http://usa.fage.eu/company/fage-story.

19. Harry A. Stark (ed.), *Ward's Automotive Yearbook 1974* (Southfield, MI: Ward's Communication, 1974).

20. *Ward's Automotive Yearbook 1989*, 1st ed. (Southfield, MI: Ward's Communication, 1989).

21. Alan K. Binder, *Ward's Automotive Yearbook 2014* (Southfield, MI: Ward's Communication, 2014).

22. Bob Drummond, "Diebold Learns What Edison Knew: Voting Machine Sales Are Tough," *Bloomberg News*, September 1, 2004.

23. Sam Walton and John Huey, *Sam Walton: Made in America* (New York: Bantam, 1993).

24. Joseph A. Schumpeter, *Capitalism, Socialism, and Democracy* (Florence, KY: Routledge Publishing, 2010).

25. Al Ries and Jack Trout, *Marketing Warfare* (New York: McGraw-Hill, 1997).

26. Anne Fisher, "Why Huge Success Can Be a Company's Worst Enemy," Fortune.com, February 2, 2013, http://fortune.com/2013/02/05/why-huge-success-can-be-a-companys-worst-enemy/.

27. "Coca-Cola Bottles: The History of Our Iconic Bottle," Coca-Cola Great Britain website (accessed February 11, 2015), www.coca-cola.co.uk/125/coca-cola-bottles-history.html.

28. Joe Sharkey, "Reinventing the Suitcase by Adding the Wheel," *New York Times*, October 4, 2010.

29. "A Brief History of Rolling Luggage," ebags.com Blog, June 29, 2009 (accessed August 10, 2015), http://blog.ebags.com/post/a-brief-history-of-rolling-luggage/.

30. Bruce Horowitz, "Success Stunned Pilot Inventor," *USA Today*, February 19, 2003.

31. L. L. Bean 2013 Company Fact Sheet, L. L. Bean website (accessed February 12, 2015), http://www.llbean.com/customerService/aboutLLBean/images/130426-fact-sheet-2013.pdf.

32. "Brain Trivia," LONI (Laboratory of Neuro Imaging) at the University of Southern California website (accessed February 11, 2015), www.loni.usc.edu/about_loni/education/brain_trivia.php.

33. Meghan Kelly, "Biggest Source of Funding for Most Startups Is Actually Surprising," Venturebeat Blog, December 3, 2013 (accessed August 10, 2015), http://finance.nbcconnecticut.com/news/venture-beat /biggest-source-of-funding-for-most-startups-is-actually-surprising/biggest -source-of-funding-for-most-startups-is-actually-surprising-12285638 .htm.

34. "Funding Your Startup: How to Get It Done," Fundable.com (accessed February 12, 2015), https://www.fundable.com/learn/resources /guides/startup-guide/funding-your-startup.

Chapter 2

1. Al Ries, Jack Trout, and Philip Kotler, *Positioning: The Battle for Your Mind* (New York: McGraw-Hill, 2000).

2. "Powering Growth through Direct Store Delivery," Grocery Manufacturers Association (GMA) report, September 2008 (accessed August 10, 2015), http://www.gmaonline.org/downloads/research-and-reports /DSD_Final_111108.pdf.

3. "Perceived Value Definition," Investopedia.com (accessed February 2, 2015), http://www.investopedia.com/terms/v/value.asp.

Chapter 3

1. "What Is Sustainability?" U.S. Environmental Protection Agency website (accessed February 2, 2015), http://epa.gov/sustainability/basic info.htm.

2. "First-Mover Definition," Investopedia.com (accessed February 15, 2015), http://www.investopedia.com/terms/f/firstmover.asp.

3. Bernie Monegain, "Ingenix Applies Quicken Way," Healthcareit news.com, May 4, 2006, http://www.healthcareitnews.com/news/ingenix -applies-quicken-way.

4. "Apple Becomes First Company Worth $700b," *The Guardian*, November 25, 2014, http://www.theguardian.com/technology/2014/nov /25/apple-first-company-worth-700bn-iphone.

Chapter 6

1. Warren Bennis and Burt Nanus, *Leaders: Strategies for Taking Charge* (New York: Harper Collins, 1985), 4.

2. Tom Peters, *In Search of Excellence: Lessons from America's Best-Run Companies* (New York: HarperBusiness, 2006).

3. Douglas McGregor, *The Human Side of Enterprise* (New York: McGraw-Hill, 1960).

4. Chester Barnard, *The Functions of the Executive: 30th Anniversary Edition* (Boston: Harvard University Press, 1971).

Chapter 7

1. Max Weber, *Economy and Society* (Berkeley: University of California Press, 1978).

2. Chester Barnard, *The Functions of the Executive: 30th Anniversary Edition* (Boston: Harvard University Press, 1971).

3. James R. Evans and William M. Lindsay, *The Management and Control of Quality*, 4th ed. (Minneapolis: West Publishing), 112.

4. W. Edwards Deming, *Out of the Crisis* (Cambridge, MA: MIT Press, 2000), 23.

Chapter 8

1. J. Max Robbins, "Oprah's OWN Makeover: From Failure to Success," *Forbes*, February 12, 2013.

2. Chris Witherspoon, "Oprah Winfrey Network Scores Best Ratings Ever Thanks to African-American Women," thegrio.com, April 1, 2014, http://thegrio.com/2014/04/01/oprah-winfrey-network-scores-best-ratings-ever-thanks-to-african-american-women.

3. Julie Creswell and Landon Thomas Jr., "The Talented Mr. Madoff," *New York Times*, January 24, 2009.

4. "Six Scholars Comparison," Department of Management Science and Engineering, Stanford University (accessed August 20, 2014), http://web.stanford.edu/class/msande269/six_scholars_comparison.html.

5. W. Edwards Deming, *Out of the Crisis* (Cambridge, MA: MIT Press, 2000).

6. Jeffrey Pfeffer and Robert I. Sutton, *Hard Facts, Dangerous Half-Truths and Total Nonsense: Profiting from Evidence-Based Management* (Boston: Harvard Review Press, 2006).

7. You can find that research at:

Angelo Mastrangelo, Erik R. Eddy, and Steven J. Lorenzet (2004), "The Importance of Personal and Professional Leadership," *Leadership & Organization Development Journal*, Vol. 25, no. 5, 435–451.

Erik R. Eddy, Steven J. Lorenzet, and Angelo Mastrangelo (2008), "Personal and Professional Leadership in a Government Agency," *Leadership & Organization Development Journal*, Vol. 29, no. 5, 412–426.

Angelo Mastrangelo, Erik R. Eddy, and Steven J. Lorenzet (2014), "The Relationship Between Enduring Leadership and Organizational Performance," *Leadership & Organization Development Journal*, Vol. 35, no. 7, 590–604.

Chapter 9

1. Chester Barnard, *The Functions of the Executive* (Cambridge, MA: Harvard University Press, 1971), 272–273.
2. "Our Credo," Johnson & Johnson website (accessed February 2, 2015), http://www.jnj.com/sites/default/files/pdf/jnj_ourcredo_english _us_8.5x11_cmyk.pdf.

Chapter 10

1. Robert H. Haveman, *Poverty Policy and Poverty Research* (Madison: University of Wisconsin Press, 1997).
2. "Bright Horizons Children's Centers, Inc.—1987," Harvard Business School Case Collection, July 1993, 2.
3. John Sawhill and David Williamson, "Measuring What Matters in Nonprofits," McKinsey & Company "Insights and Publications" website (accessed February 2015), http://www.mckinsey.com/insights /social_sector/measuring_what_matters_in_nonprofits.
4. Richard Larkin, "Using Outcomes to Measure Nonprofit Success," *Nonprofit Quarterly*, February 2, 2013. https://nonprofitquarterly .org/management/22549-using-outcomes-to-measure-nonprofit-success .html.
5. James Austin, Howard Stevenson, and Jane Wei-Skillern, "Social and Commercial Entrepreneurship: Different, or Both," *Journal of Marketing*, 2005.

Chapter 11

1. "The Pacific Railway: A Brief History of Building the Transcontinental Railroad," Linda Hall Library website (accessed February 11, 2015), http://railroad.lindahall.org/essays/brief-history.html.
2. David Herbert Donald, *Lincoln* (New York: Simon & Schuster, 1995).
3. "The Pacific Railway: A Brief History of Building the Transcontinental Railroad," Linda Hall Library website (accessed February 11, 2015), http://railroad.lindahall.org/essays/brief-history.html.

4. "The Great Depression," Ithaca College Department of History website (accessed July 28, 2015), http://faculty.ithaca.edu/mismith/docs /USsince1865/depression.pdf.

5. "Life During the Depression," Marquette University History Department website (accessed July 28, 2015), http://academic.mu.edu /meissnerd/depression.htm.

6. "Inaugural Address of the President," National Archives website (accessed July 28, 2015), http://www.archives.gov/education/lessons/fdr -inaugural/images/address-1.gif

7. Richard E. Neustadt, *Presidential Power: The Politics of Leadership from FDR to Carter* (New York: John Wiley & Sons, 1980), 119.

8. William D. Pederson, *A Companion to Franklin D. Roosevelt* (New York: John Wiley & Sons, 2011).

9. "Franklin D. Roosevelt (FDR): First 100 Days," Schmoop.com (accessed February 2, 2015), http://shmoop.com/franklin-d-roosevelt -fdr/first-100-days.html.

10. Wayne D. Rasmussen, Gladys L. Baker, and James S. Ward, *A Short History of Agricultural Adjustment, 1933–1975* (Washington: Economic Research Service, U.S. Department of Agriculture, 1976).

11. "Remembering Franklin Delano Roosevelt," *Washington Post* website (accessed February 2, 2015), http://www.washingtonpost.com /wp-srv/local/longterm/tours/fdr/remembrances.htm.

12. "Transcript of National Interstate and Defense Highways Act (1956)," Ourdocuments.gov (accessed February 2, 2015), http://www .ourdocuments.gov/doc.php?doc=88&page=transcript.

13. Brandon Keim, "June 29, 1956: Ike Signs Interstate Highway Act," Wired.com, June 29, 2010, http://www.wired.com/2010/06/0629 interstate-highway-act/.

14. "Entrepreneurship: A Working Definition," *Harvard Business Review* Blog, January 10, 2013.

15. Peter D. Schiff and John Downes, *Crash Proof: How to Profit From the Coming Economic Collapse* (New York: Wiley, 2007).

16. "Former TARP Watchdog: 'We're Headed Toward Another Financial Crisis,' " WBUR-Boston, September 13, 2013, http://hereand now.wbur.org/2013/09/13/tarp-watchdog-banks.

Chapter 12

1. Harlan D. Plat, *Why Companies Fail: Strategies for Detecting, Avoiding, and Profiting from Bankruptcy* (New York: Lexington Books, 1985).

2. Stephen R. Covey, *The 7 Habits of Highly Effective People: Powerful Lessons for Personal Change* (New York: Free Press, 2004), 236–240.

3. Charles Cooper, "Growing Pains," *America's Best,* July/August 2009.

4. John C. Maxwell Jr., "The Maxwell Consumer Report," February 3, 1994.

5. "Beverage Industry: Celebrating 50 Years of Service," Library of Congress: American Memory website (accessed August 10, 2015), http://memory.loc.gov/ammem/ccmphtml/indsthst.html.

6. Charles Dickens, *David Copperfield* (New York: Penguin Classics, 2004).

7. Barbara Pinckney, "The Sad End of the Al Lawrence Story," *Albany Business Journal,* January 21, 2012, http://www.bizjournals.com/albany/stories/2002/01/21/editorial1.html.

8. Dennis Yusko, "No Fairy Tale Life within Walls: Feds Allege Woman Is Victim of Dawn to Dusk Forced Labor at Mansion," *Albany Times-Union,* March 2, 2012 (accessed August 10, 2015), http://www.timesunion.com/local/article/No-fairy-tale-life-within-walls-3373942.php.

Chapter 14

1. "Calvin Coolidge—Quotes—Quotable Quote," Goodreads (accessed February 2, 2015), http://www.goodreads.com/quotes/2749-nothing-in-the-world-can-take-the-place-of-persistence.

Chapter 15

1. "General Article: Domestic Politics—Reagan," PBS website (accessed February 2, 2015), http://www.pbs.org/wgbh/americanexperience/features/general-article/reagan-domestic/.

2. "Remarks by the President at Morehouse College Commencement Ceremony," The White House, Office of the Press Secretary, May 19, 2013 (accessed August 1, 2015), https://www.whitehouse.gov/the-press-office/2013/05/19/remarks-president-morehouse-college-commencement-ceremony.

Bibliography

Austin, James, Howard Stevenson, and Jane Wei-Skillern. "Social and Commercial Entrepreneurship: Different, or Both," *Journal of Marketing*, 2005.

Barnard, Chester. *The Functions of the Executive: 30th Anniversary Edition*. Cambridge, MA: Harvard University Press, 1971.

Bennis, Warren, and Burt Nanus. *Leaders: Strategies for Taking Charge*. New York: Harper Collins, 1985.

Covey, Stephen R. *The 7 Habits of Highly Effective People: Powerful Lessons for Personal Change*. New York: Free Press, 2004.

Deming, W. Edwards. *Out of the Crisis*. Cambridge, MA: MIT Press, 2000.

Dickens, Charles. *David Copperfield*. New York: Penguin Classics, 2004.

Drucker, Peter F. *Innovation and Entrepreneurship*. New York: HarperBusiness, 2006.

Evans, James R., and William M. Lindsay. *The Management and Control of Quality*, 4th ed. Minneapolis: West Publishing, 1988.

Ford, Henry. *My Life and Work*. Standard Publications, 2006.

Havemen, Robert H. *Poverty Policy and Poverty Research*. Madison: University of Wisconsin Press, 1997.

McGregor, Douglas. *The Human Side of Enterprise*. New York: McGraw-Hill, 1960.

Neustadt, Richard E. *Presidential Power: The Politics of Leadership from FDR to Carter*. New York: John Wiley & Sons, 1980.

Pederson, William D. *A Companion to Franklin D. Roosevelt*. New York: John Wiley & Sons, 2011.

Peters, Tom. *In Search of Excellence: Lessons from America's Best-Run Companies*. New York: HarperBusiness, 2006.

Pfeffer, Jeffrey, and Robert I. Sutton. *Hard Facts, Dangerous Half-Truths and Total Nonsense: Profiting from Evidence-Based Management.* Boston: Harvard Review Press, 2006.

Plat, Harlan D. *Why Companies Fail: Strategies for Detecting, Avoiding, and Profiting from Bankruptcy.* New York: Lexington Books, 1985.

Rasmussen, Wayne D., Gladys L. Baker, and James S. Ward. *A Short History of Agricultural Adjustment, 1933–1935.* Washington: Economic Research Service, U.S. Department of Agriculture, 1976.

Ries, Al, and Jack Trout. *Marketing Warfare.* New York: McGraw-Hill, 1997.

Ries, Al, Jack Trout, and Philip Kotler. *Positioning: The Battle for Your Mind.* New York: McGraw-Hill, 2000.

Schiff, Peter D., and John Downs. *Crash Proof: How to Profit from the Coming Economic Collapse.* New York: Wiley, 2007.

Schumpeter, Joseph A. *Capitalism, Socialism, and Democracy,* new ed. Start Publishing, 2012.

Schumpeter, Joseph A. *The Theory of Economic Development: An Inquiry into Profits, Capital, Credit, Interest, and the Business Cycle.* Edison, NJ: Transaction Publishers, 1982.

Walton, Sam, and John Huey. *Sam Walton: Made in America.* New York: Bantam, 1993.

Ward's Automotive Yearbook 1989. Southfield, MI: Ward's Communications, 1989.

Ward's Automotive Yearbook 2014. Southfield, MI: Ward's Communications, 1989.

Weber, Max. *Economy and Society.* Berkeley: University of California Press, 1978.

Index

About the Author

PROFESSOR ANGELO MASTRANGELO'S business career followed a pathway most think is possible only in fictional odes to the American dream. After starting out as stock boy and then working as a milkman in New York State in the 1960s, Mastrangelo landed a job as a salesman at Canada Dry of Southern New York, without any college education. He rose through the ranks to become Canada Dry's sales supervisor and was quickly promoted to general manager at Bev-Pak, Inc., a company owned by Touhey Associates.

Seven years later, after working as plant manager at C&C Cola (formerly Bev-Pak), a division of ITT, Mastrangelo purchased Bev-Pak in 1980 and renamed it Adirondack Beverages. He then led a bold turnaround, increasing the company's sales by 500 percent at a time of industry-wide crisis. Four years prior to selling Adirondack Beverages to the investment bank Dillon Reed, Mastrangelo implemented new companywide TQM, or total quality management, programs.

These earned Adirondack Beverages several local and regional awards, including the Top Ten Award for Outstanding Companies in the Capital District by the Albany Chamber of Commerce. Many of Mastrangelo's TQM programs are still in place today—a testament to him weathering the "Cola Wars" with courage, grace, and long-ranging wisdom.

After attending the highly regarded Owner/President Management (OPM) program at Harvard Business School, Mastrangelo decided to explore the "theoretical" reasons for his real-world successes. He entered into the organizational studies PhD program at Albany University in 1994 and earned his degree in 2000. In 2001, he began teaching leadership and entrepreneurship at Binghamton University. In 2007 he was named as one of the top entrepreneurship professors in the United States by Fortune Small Business. Since 1987, Mastrangelo's Second Chance Scholarship Foundation has helped more than 1,400 local students go to college.